CA Proficiency 2

FINANCIAL REPORTING TOOLKIT

CA Proficiency 2

FINANCIAL REPORTING TOOLKIT

Published in 2011 by
Chartered Accountants Ireland
Chartered Accountants House
47–49 Pearse Street
Dublin 2
www.charteredaccountants.ie

First published 2008; updated 2009 and 2011

This publication is designed to provide accurate and authoritative information in regard to the subject matter covered. It is provided on the understanding that the Institute of Chartered Accountants in Ireland is not engaged in rendering professional services. The Institute of Chartered Accountants in Ireland disclaims all liability for any reliance placed on the information contained within this publication and recommends that if professional advice or other expert assistance is required, the services of a competent professional should be sought.

ISBN: 978-1-907214-70-7

Typeset by Hurix
Printed by Turners Printing

CONTENTS

COMMON ABBREVIATIONS

CSCI	Consolidated Statement of Comprehensive Income
CSFP	Consolidated Statement of Financial Position
IAS	International Accounting Standard
IASB	International Accounting Standards Board
IASC	International Accounting Standards Committee
JNL	Journal
IFRS	International Financial Reporting Standard
NA	Net Assets
NCI	Non-controlling Interest
PAT	Profit After Tax
PBT	Profit Before Tax
RE	Retained Earnings
SCI	Statement of Comprehensive Income
SFP	Statement of Financial Position
TB	Trial Balance

As part of the CA Proficiency 2 course, you are invited here to take on the role of James Crown, a trainee accountant in the firm of Sonner & Saville, Chartered Accountants. Throughout the period of your studies, you will be asked by the relevant partner in the firm to carry out tasks which simulate real-life situations. These tasks are designed to help you to acquire the knowledge and competencies that you will require in order to be successful in your professional examinations.

Throughout the Toolkit, reference is made to your core financial accounting text, *International Financial Accounting and Reporting* (3rd Edition) by Ciaran Connolly, referred to in this Toolkit as ***Connolly***[1]. The references indicate the pre-requisite reading and study necessary in order to gain an understanding of a particular topic. These references also direct you to questions that you should attempt in exam-simulated circumstances.

---

[1] Connolly, C. (2011), *International Financial Accounting and Reporting*, 3rd Edition, Dublin: Chartered Accountants Ireland.

INTRODUCTION

The purpose of this Toolkit is to equip students with an understanding of the context of financial reporting in the business environment. It consists of four 'sessions' which address the main elements of the CAP 2 Financial Reporting Syllabus. The broad structure of the Toolkit is as follows:

- Session One – Introductory Issues – addresses some fundamental accounting principles that underlie financial reporting and the preparation of financial statements;
- Session Two – Preparation of Company Financial Statements – concentrates on the core IFRSs associated with the preparation and presentation of financial statements for a single company;
- Session Three – Analysis and Interpretation of Financial Statements – focuses on understanding published financial information; and
- Session Four – Preparation of Consolidated Financial Statements – deals with accounting for business combinations.

Each session, which addresses elements of the three topic areas included in the Financial Reporting Competency Statement, consists of a series of meetings, and subsequent tasks, with the Audit Partner, John Keane. Suggested solutions to each of the tasks are provided at the end of this Toolkit. The sessions and tasks are designed to imitate the real life experiences of a trainee chartered accountant in practice and to help you pass the CAP 2 Financial Reporting examination. Learning objectives and outcomes are clearly stated for each session, together with the expected 'competency level' (as per the CAP 2 Financial Reporting Syllabus). Additional background reading and relevant practice questions included in the course text[2] are cross-referenced throughout each session.

Please note that the exercises or 'tasks' that form part of this Toolkit are not designed to replicate the style or length of the CAP 2 Financial Reporting examination, but are written so as to help achieve the prescribed Learning Outcomes which are set out below. While the tasks are of an appropriate standard for the CAP 2 Financial Reporting examination, many are more comprehensive and time consuming than an exam question on the same topic.

---

[2] Connolly, C. (2011), *International Financial Accounting and Reporting*, 3rd Edition, Dublin: Chartered Accountants Ireland.

This Toolkit has been fully revised to reflect the requirements of all extant International Accounting Standards (IASs) and International Financial Reporting Standards (IFRSs) as at 1 June 2011. It is designed to assist students with the development of their knowledge and skills so as to enable them to appraise underlying accounting concepts and apply extant IASs and IFRSs. IFRS terminology is applied throughout this text (for example: statement of financial position (not balance sheet); statement of comprehensive income (not income statement); and statement of cash flows (not cash flow statement). In order to be consistent with the practice applied for examinations, the tasks and questions included in this Toolkit are denominated in '€/£'.

Finally, remember that practice makes perfect so please attempt this Toolkit, together with numerous past paper questions, as often as possible during the course of your studies.

BACKGROUND

You are James Crown and you have just completed your undergraduate degree, graduating with a 2.1. You have always wanted to be a Chartered Accountant and you have been offered a training contract with Saville & Sonner, Chartered Accountants, a highly respected firm that you believe can provide a wide breadth of experience throughout the period of your training.

George Saville retired some years ago, and Jeanne Sonner is the managing partner, having taken over from her father who has also now retired. There are four other partners in the firm:

Kim Lu	Harry O'Neill	John Keane	Brenda Perry
Taxation Partner	Corporate Finance Partner	Audit Partner	Professional Standards Partner

Your training will provide you with experience in each of these areas.

When you arrived in Sonner & Saville, Chartered Accountants you were pleased to discover that Catherine Clarke, whom you knew vaguely from your college days, is also a trainee Chartered Accountant with the firm. Catherine is sitting her finals this autumn.

In your first week in the office the partners want you to simply familiarise yourself with the Sonner & Saville way of doing business. They also take you and, because you already know her, Catherine to lunch. During lunch, John Keane spoke on the merits on becoming a Chartered Accountant and emphasised the relationship between your training and education. He knew that you would not be very busy this week and suggested that you read the CAP 2 Competency Statement, in particular those aspects relating to Paper 3 Financial Reporting published by Chartered Accountants Ireland. He also reminded you that a strong theoretical understanding of financial reporting will be required to carry out your work during your training contract and that this Statement forms the basis for the structure and content of the Financial Reporting examination.

Competency Levels

Now that you have read the Financial Reporting Competency Statement, you should have a broad understanding of what will be expected of you in the examination. In respect of each competency, candidates are expected to attain a specific level. The competency levels expected for the CAP 2 Financial Reporting examination are a combination of 'U', 'A' and 'I'. These can be defined as follows:

- Understanding (U) – a comprehension of the fundamental concepts of the topic and an awareness of their impact in resolving problems;
- Application (A) – a comprehension of the fundamental concepts of the topic and the ability to bring that comprehension to bear in resolving problems where data is provided in a structured form; and
- Integration (I) – a detailed comprehension of core concepts and principles and the capability to apply this comprehension along with professional judgement to the resolution of problems in both an intra and inter-disciplinary context.

So now you are all set, turn the page and commence the first session.

Good Luck!

Session One

INTRODUCTORY ISSUES

On successful completion of this session, you should understand:

- the objectives of financial reporting;
- the desirable characteristics of financial reports;
- the regulatory framework;
- what is meant by a conceptual framework and the need for such a framework; and
- the detailed disclosure requirements of IAS 1 *Preparation of Financial Statements*, including the illustrative formats.

Competency Level: Integration.
It is your second week in Saville, Sonner & Co, Chartered Accountants. It is the middle of October, the nights are getting long and university seems a lifetime ago. However, you have settled in well and are about to commence your first financial reporting assignment.

Meeting 1.1

In advance of your first meeting with the Audit Partner, John Keane, he advised you to read the following chapter from the course text:

Required Study

Connolly: **Chapter 1** – Framework for Financial Reporting (excluding Section 1.4 Fair Value Measurement)

Self-test Questions
1. What is relevance?
2. What is objectivity?
3. What is a conceptual framework?
4. Outline the contents of the chapters that comprise the *IFRS Framework*.
5. Describe the three levels in the fair value hierarchy and the three different approaches to determining fair value.

During the meeting, you discovered the following information:

- The firm recently acquired a new client, Holinwall Limited (Holinwall). Holinwall is involved in the development and use of fibre optic technology, particularly in the telecommunications and banking industries. The company, which has decided to prepare its financial statements to 31 December each year, commenced trading on 1 January 2011, and their first set of financial statements will be for the year ended 31 December 2011; and
- Holinwall, which was purchased as an 'off the shelf' company, has a total authorised share capital of €/£1,000,000, consisting of 600,000 €/£1 ordinary shares and 200,000 5% €/£2 cumulative redeemable preference shares. The issued share capital is currently one €/£1 ordinary share, and this is held by one of the three directors, Chris Holinwall. The other two directors, Caiti Grant and Ellen McQuillan, are, like Chris, from an engineering background. While all the appropriate legal and statutory requirements were complied with, the formation of the company was somewhat hurried in order that it could commence trading. Consequently, a number of issues and queries were 'put on the back burner'. Furthermore, Holinwall has had to rely on your firm for accounting advice as the company has been unable to recruit a finance director and currently only employs an unqualified book-keeper on a part-time basis.

As, similar to yourself, Holinwall is a new company just beginning what will hopefully be a long and successful relationship with the firm, John Keane believes that it would be an ideal client for you to become involved with.

Task 1.1

Obtain the financial statements for any three different companies. Identify the types of shares in issue for the chosen companies from the financial statements and supporting notes. Prepare a letter, for approval by John Keane, addressed to the directors of Holinwall that explains the key features of, and the differences between, ordinary share capital and preference share capital.

Task 1.2

Holinwall wishes to raise €/£800,000 in capital to help fund expansion plans. Include in the letter referred to above (see Task 1.1), the number of ordinary and preference shares that the company should issue to minimise the preference dividend payment in each of the following circumstances (you may ignore the one share already issued and held by Chris Holinwall):

1. All shares are issued at par; and
2. The ordinary shares are issued at a premium of 25 c/p and the preference shares at a premium of 50 c/p.

Meeting 1.2

Connolly: **Chapter 2** – Presentation of Financial Statements

Self-test Questions (at the end of that chapter)
1. What are the main principles of financial reporting?
2. What are the components of a complete set of financial statements?
3. What criteria determine whether assets should be classified as current or non-current?
4. What criteria determine whether liabilities should be classified as current or non-current?
5. What minimum information should be presented in the statement of comprehensive income?
6. Distinguish between the function of expenditure and nature of expenditure methods of classifying expenses in the statement of comprehensive income.

In mid-November 2011, John Keane met with the directors of Holinwall over lunch to discuss the preparation and audit of the company's 2011 financial statements. Shortly afterwards, he called you into his office and handed you a grubby napkin containing some notes that he had taken during the lunch.

Task 1.3

The directors of Holinwall recently attended a seminar on the rights and duties of company directors. The directors were surprised to discover that:

(a) company law requires that directors: maintain proper accounting records; and prepare annual financial statements, including a directors' report, and make these available to shareholders and the public at large; and
(b) IAS 1 *Presentation of Financial Statements* does not state that the overriding requirement is for financial statements to show a 'correct' or 'accurate' presentation of a company.

Prepare a letter, for approval by John Keane, addressed to the directors of Holinwall explaining why directors are required to account in this way and who benefits from these requirements.

Telephone Call 1.1

Required Study

Connolly: **Chapter 6** – Property, Plant and Equipment

Self-test Questions (at the end of that chapter)
1. What elements of expenditure are included in the production cost of a non-current asset?
2. What disclosures are required when a non-current asset is revalued?
3. In what circumstances may an amount be transferred from the revaluation reserve to a credit on the statement of comprehensive income?
4. What is depreciation?
5. What accounting treatment is required if the estimated useful life of a fixed asset is revised?

Pleased with the style and content of your draft letters, John Keane left instructions that if he was unavailable then telephone calls from Holinwall with respect to audit and accounting issues could be transferred initially to you.

Late one Friday afternoon in early December 2011, Holinwall's book-keeper telephoned in a panic. Chris Holinwall had purchased a new motor car for himself through the company and had handed the invoice to the book-keeper before leaving for the weekend and asking the book-keeper to arrange for the dealership to be paid. The invoice revealed:

	€/£
New Audi TT	40,000
Delivery charge	200
Alloy wheels	1,500
Sunroof	1,800
Petrol	100
Number plates	150
Road fund licence	250
	44,000
Part exchange – Reliant Robin	(2,000)
Amount due	42,000

Task 1.4

The book-keeper asked for your advice on how to account for the purchase of the new car and the disposal of the Reliant Robin. He informed you that the Reliant Robin was purchased by Holinwall in January 2011 for €/£3,000 cash. Prepare an e-mail, for approval by John Keane, addressed to Holinwall's book-keeper that explains clearly how the acquisition and disposal of the motor cars should be accounted for.

Meeting 1.3

Required Study

Connolly: **Chapter 4** – Revenue Recognition

Self-test Questions (at the end of that chapter)
1. At what value should revenue be measured?
2. What conditions must be met before revenue from the sale of goods may be recognised?
3. What conditions must be met before revenue from the delivery of services may be recognised?

The directors of Holinwall decided to close the company for two weeks over the Christmas period. Consequently, it was decided to conduct the year-end inventory count prior to the Christmas holidays.

While attending the year-end inventory count, Chris Holinwall gave you a tour of the company's offices and research facilities. Over coffee he enthusiastically explained further the nature of the company's activities and its plans for the future. After joking about the similarities between your boss and his famous brother, Chris showed you a recent newspaper article that referred to 'creative accounting'.

Task 1.5

Explain what is meant by the term 'creative accounting' and why companies might engage in it?

Telephone Call 1.2

Connolly: **Chapter 6** – Property, Plant and Equipment

Self-test Questions (at the end of that chapter)
1. What elements of expenditure are included in the production cost of a non-current asset?
2. What disclosures are required when a non-current asset is revalued?
3. In what circumstances may an amount be transferred from the revaluation reserve to the credit of the statement of comprehensive income?
4. What is depreciation?
5. What accounting treatment is required if the estimated useful life of a non-current asset is revised?

Shortly before finishing for the Christmas holidays, Holinwall's book-keeper telephoned to ask for your advice on how to deal with two issues.

First, he informed you that he was working on the preparations for extracting a trial balance as at 31 December 2011 and explained that Holinwall's non-current assets consisted of land, property, plant, equipment and motor vehicles. The book-keeper indicated that one of the company's directors had suggested that it might be more meaningful to record some of the company's non-current assets at valuation rather than historical cost.

Secondly, he told you that the directors of Holinwall have been involved in negotiations with the official representatives of a foreign bank about the feasibility of Holinwall being asked to tender for a contract to replace the fibre optic cabling in their Irish offices. The negotiations began in early 2011 and are now at an advanced stage. The award of the contract would help secure the long-term future of Holinwall and could lead to further similar business opportunities. The next major round of negotiations is due to take place before the end of 2011 and Holinwall's directors are considering presenting the foreign representatives with some gifts in recognition of the good relations that have developed during the negotiations and also to help conclude the deal.

Task 1.6

Prepare a letter, for approval by John Keane, addressed to Holinwall's book-keeper that:

(a) explains the circumstances when recording a non-current asset at historical cost might not be relevant to users of financial statements; and
(b) advises the directors on the ethical considerations associated with their proposal to offer gifts to the foreign bank's representatives.

And finally.

Just before you leave for your well-earned Christmas holidays, Catherine Clarke calls by with a present – a list of questions that she believes would be useful for you to attempt before progressing to Session Two:

Connolly: **Chapter 1** – Framework for Financial Reporting
Review Questions* 1.1–1.3
Challenging Questions* 1.1–1.3

Connolly: **Chapter 2** – Presentation of Financial Statements
Review Questions 2.1 and 2.2
Challenging Questions 2.1 and 2.2

Connolly: **Chapter 4** – Revenue Recognition
Review Question 4.1
Challenging Question 4.1

Connolly: **Chapter 6** – Property, Plant and Equipment
Review Questions 6.1 and 6.2
Challenging Questions 6.1 and 6.2

* Note: Review Questions and Challenging Questions are in the QUESTIONS section at the end of each chapter.

She strongly stresses to you the importance of attempting these questions under examination conditions in the appropriate time.

Congratulations, you have now finished Session One. Relax, take a (short) break and when you are ready, begin Session Two which focuses on the preparation of company financial statements.

SESSION TWO

PREPARATION OF COMPANY FINANCIAL STATEMENTS

On successful completion of this session, you should:

- understand the principles of (specified) International Financial Reporting Standards (IFRSs);
- be able to demonstrate an ability to apply these IFRSs to a specified range of business transactions; and
- be competent to prepare and present the published financial statements of individual companies.

Competency Level: Integration.

Required Study

Connolly: Chapter 7 – Borrowing Costs

Self-test Questions
1. What are the arguments for and against the capitalisation of borrowing costs?
2. What is the accounting treatment for qualifying borrowing costs?
3. When may capitalisation of borrowing costs begin and when must it end?

Connolly: Chapter 8 – Leases

Self-test Questions
1. What is the difference between a finance and an operating lease?
2. With respect to a finance lease, what should you show in the statement of financial position of the lessee?
3. With respect to a finance lease, how do you account for the rental payments from the lessee's point of view?
4. What is the preferred method of apportioning the rental repayments between the interest and capital element?
5. List the disclosure requirements for both operating and finance leases.

Connolly: Chapter 9 – Intangible Assets

Self-test Questions

1. Under IAS 38, what are the categories of internally generated intangible assets which may never be recognised?
2. What criteria must be satisfied before development expenditure may be capitalised?
3. If all the conditions in the previous question are met, is it a requirement that development costs must be capitalised?

Connolly: Chapter 10 – Impairment

Self-test Questions

1. Define the term 'impairment loss'.
2. Define the term 'cash generating unit'.
3. List the factors which suggest that an asset may have been impaired.
4. Explain how the recoverable amount of an asset is determined.

Connolly: Chapter 11 – Inventories

Self-test Questions

1. How should inventory be measured in accordance with IAS 2?
2. What does the cost of inventory comprise?
3. Name and describe two methods identified in IAS 2 for the measurement of cost.

Connolly: Chapter 14 – Provisions, Contingent Liabilities and Contingent Assets

Self-test Questions

1. How does IAS 37 define a provision?
2. According to IAS 37, when, and only when, can a provision be recognised?
3. Can a provision ever be made for future operating losses?
4. How does IAS 37 define a contingent liability?
5. When should a contingent liability be recognised?

Connolly: Chapter 15 – Events After the Reporting Period

Self-test Questions

1. What is an event after the end of the reporting period?
2. What is an adjusting event?
3. Give three examples of an adjusting event.
4. Give three examples of a non-adjusting event.
5. In what circumstances will a non-adjusting event require changes in the amounts to be disclosed in the financial statements?

Connolly: Chapter 16 – Accounting for Government Grants and Disclosure of Government Assistance

Self-test Questions

1. How should grants related to income be accounted for?
2. What are the two allowable methods of accounting for grants related to assets?
3. What is the disclosure requirement listed in IAS 20?
4. When and how should potential liabilities to repay grants be accounted for?

Connolly: Chapter 20 – Non-Current Assets Held for Sale and Discontinued Operations

Self-test Questions

1. What is a discontinued operation?
2. What information must be disclosed in the financial statements for discontinued operations?

Connolly: Chapter 22 – Related Party Disclosures

Self-test Questions

1. In the context of IAS 24, what are the main parties to which a company may be related?
2. What are the disclosures required by IAS 24 with respect to related parties?

Connolly: Chapter 25 – Financial Investments

In particular, please ensure that you understand whether a financial investment should be classified as debt or equity and the consequences of this (see Section 25.2).

Self-test Questions

1. Define the terms 'financial instrument', 'financial asset', 'financial liability', 'equity instrument' and 'derivative'.
2. Explain the difference between financial liabilities and equity.
3. Explain how preference shares should be accounted for in accordance with IAS 32.
4. Identify and explain the four categories of financial asset outlined in IAS 39.
5. Explain the terms 'credit risk', 'liquidity risk' and 'market risk' in the context of IFRS 7, and outline the main disclosure required in relation to each of these risks.

Connolly: Chapter 31 – Foreign Currency Transactions and Translation of Foreign Operations (*Transactions only*)

Question 31.1

IAS 21 *The Effects of Changes in Foreign Exchange Rates* defines the functional currency as the currency:

(a) in which the foreign operation measures and records its transactions.
(b) of the primary economic environment in which the entity operates.

(c) in which the financial statements are presented.
(d) of the country in which the subsidiary is located.

Question 31.2

According to IAS 21 *The Effects of Changes in Foreign Exchange Rates* the following statement 'the currency that affects the economic wealth of the entity' provides a definition of:

(a) functional currency.
(b) local currency.
(c) presentation currency.
(d) foreign currency.

Question 31.3

According to IAS 21 *The Effects of Changes in Foreign Exchange Rates* the currency in which an entity primarily generates and expends cash is considered to be the:

(a) economic currency.
(b) domestic currency.
(c) presentation currency.
(d) functional currency.

Solutions to Self-Test Questions: Question 31.1 (b); 31.2 (a); 31.3 (d)

It is early February 2012 and you have spent the previous 3-4 weeks attending inventory counts and helping other colleagues with ad hoc audit tasks. However, you now have the opportunity to continue your involvement with Holinwall.

Holinwall's book-keeper has prepared a trial balance as at 31 December 2011, and a number of issues are still to be resolved before the financial statements for the year ended 31 December 2011 can be finalised.

Holinwall
Draft Trial Balance as at 31 December 2011

	Note	DR €/£	CR €/£
Revenue			20,000,000
Purchases of raw materials		8,000,000	
Production overheads (excluding direct cost of raw materials)	8	2,000,000	

Administrative expenses		2,500,000	
Selling and distribution costs	6, 10	1,100,000	
Finance costs	3	250,000	
€/£1 ordinary shares			600,000
Share premium – ordinary shares			150,000
5% €/£2 cumulative redeemable preference shares			40,000
Share premium – preference shares			10,000
Land – cost at 31 December 2011	2	1,000,000	
Property – cost at 31 December 2011		2,500,000	
Property – accumulated depreciation at 31 December 2011	13		–
Plant and equipment – cost at 31 December 2011	1, 4	700,000	
Plant and equipment – accumulated depreciation at 31 December 2011	13		–
Motor vehicles – cost at 31 December 2011		120,000	
Motor vehicles – accumulated depreciation at 31 December 2011	13		–
Research expenditure	7	3,500,000	
Trade receivables		1,200,000	
Other receivables and prepayments		260,000	
Bank and cash		180,000	
Trade payables			1,240,000
Other payables and accruals	5		270,000
Bank borrowings – current			250,000
Bank borrowings – non-current			750,000
		23,310,000	23,310,000

Additional Information:

1. The directors of Holinwall conducted an impairment review of all the company's non-current assets included in the draft trial balance at 31 December 2011. The directors believe that due to the rapidly changing technological nature of their business one of the services that the company provides may no longer be profitable. The following information has been prepared with respect to the service's non-current assets:

Gross market value of plant and equipment	€/£250,000
Book value of plant and equipment	€/£400,000
Selling costs	€/£25,000
Direct future cash flows	€/£30,000 per annum for 8 years
Central overheads (excluding depreciation)	€/£40,000
Head office assets	€/£1,000,000
Weighted average cost of capital	8%

Overheads may be apportioned on a square meter basis and the service's non-current assets occupy approximately 10% of total floor space.

2. In December 2011, as part of plans to improve north-south rail links, the government announced its intention to place a compulsory purchase order on land that Holinwall had purchased in January 2011 for €/£500,000. Experience with similar compulsory purchase orders suggests that the government will purchase the land for 1½ times its original purchase price. No adjustment has yet been made for this in the 2011 financial statements, and the €/£500,000 original purchase cost is included in the €/£1,000,000 cost of land included in the draft trial balance at 31 December 2011.

3. During the year ended 31 December 2011, Holinwall extended its inventory storage facilities at a cost of €/£2,000,000. The work began in January 2011 and was completed in December 2011. The €/£2,000,000 extension cost is included in the €/£2,500,000 cost of property at 31 December 2011 shown in the draft trial balance at 31 December 2011. The extension was financed 50% by general funds and 50% by specific debt. Holinwall's current borrowing rate is 8% and a specific loan at 10% per annum was arranged. All interest paid and payable is included under finance costs in the draft trial balance at 31 December 2011.

4. Holinwall purchased computer equipment under a three-year agreement commencing in April 2011. Under the terms of the agreement Holinwall is required to make annual payments of €/£7,500 in arrears. The cost of the computer equipment would have been €/£16,500. This transaction is not reflected in the draft trial balance as at 31 December 2011.

5. Included in other payables and accruals in the draft trial balance at 31 December 2011 is an amount due to Guyere AG, a Swiss company which Holinwall purchased equipment from on 1 September 2011 for 120,000 Swiss francs (Swfr). Holinwall's bookkeeper was unaware that Holinwall had entered into a forward contract and recorded the transaction as if no forward contract existed. The exchange rates were as follows:

Forward contract rate	7.5 Swfr:€/£1
1 September 2011	8.0 Swfr:€/£1
31 December 2011	8.5 Swfr:€/£1

6. Holinwall acquired a van under a four year lease in January 2011 at a monthly rental of €/£400. The agreement requires the van to be returned to the lessor at the end of the lease period. The cost of a new van would have been €/£18,500. The 12 monthly payments for 2011 are included in selling and distribution costs in the draft trial balance at 31 December 2011.

7. As shown in the draft trial balance at 31 December 2011, Holinwall spent €/£3,500,000 on research during the year ended 31 December 2011. The directors believe that the results indicate a market for new services, together with the technical feasibility of the project. It is anticipated that sales will occur evenly during the three years 2012 to 2014. Details of the expenditure are as follows:

	Actual Expenditure	Anticipated Expenditure
	Year ended 31 December 2011	Year ended 31 December 2011
	€/£	€/£
Feasibility study	500,000	–
Initial research on service development	1,600,000	–
Expenditure on the new service	900,000	2,000,000
Plant and equipment	500,000	–
	3,500,000	2,000,000

8. The cost of Holinwall's inventory at 31 December 2011 was €/£800,000. However, this is based upon direct prime cost as the book-keeper was uncertain how to deal with overhead expenditure. As per the draft trial balance at 31 December 2011, Holinwall incurred the following overheads during the year ended 31 December 2011:

	€/£
Production overheads	2,000,000
Administrative expenses	2,500,000
Selling and distribution costs	1,100,000

The total production for the year ended 31 December 2011 was 800,000 units, which is considered normal, and the directors believe that 10% of production remains in inventory at 31 December 2011.

9. Holinwall is currently being sued for damaging the facade of a listed building when installing an ATM machine during the year ended 31 December 2011. The rectification costs are estimated to be €/£250,000, and legal advice suggest that there is greater than 50% chance that Holinwall will be found liable. The book-keeper has decided not to reflect this in the 2011 financial statements as the matter remains unresolved.

10. During the year ended 31 December 2011, Holinwall received a government grant of €/£200,000 towards the creation of 20 new selling and distribution related jobs over the period 2011 to 2013. At 31 December 2011, Holinwall had created 12 of the required new posts and the directors fully expected to create the remaining eight jobs during 2012. The grant received of €/£200,000 has been credited to selling and distribution costs in the draft trial balance at 31 December 2011.

11. Holinwall, which was purchased as an 'off the shelf' company, has a total author-ised share capital of €/£1,000,000, consisting of 600,000 €/£1 ordinary shares and 200,000 5% €/£2 cumulative redeemable preference shares. Holinwall commenced trading on 1 January 2011 with one €/£1 ordinary share in issue. This was purchased by one of the three directors, Chris Holinwall, for €/£1.25 cash. On 1 July 2011, the remainder of the €/£1 ordinary shares were issued on the same terms while 20,000 5% €/£2 cumulative redeemable preference shares were issued at €/£2.50 per share. Both the ordinary shares and the preference shares were deemed to have been issued at full market price.

The directors wish to accrue an ordinary dividend of €/£0.10 per share in issue at 31 December 2011 in the 2011 financial statements

12. One of the directors of Holinwall, Mr Right, is a partner in the legal firm of Right & Tight. The legal firm provided services for Holinwall during the year ended 31 December 2011 for which it charged fees of €/£80,000. These are included under administrative expenses in the draft trial balance as at 31 December 2011.

In addition, Holinwall purchased €/£275,000 of packaging materials from Boxit Limited at an arm's length price. This has been charged to selling and distribution costs. One of the directors of Boxit Limited, Mr Liddle, is also a director of Holin-wall. At 31 December 2011, there was €/£40,000 still outstanding and included within trade payables in the draft trial balance as at this date.

13. It is company policy to charge a full year's depreciation in the year of acquisition and none in the year of disposal. Depreciation, which is charged to administrative expenses, is calculated as follows:

Land   – nil;
Property   – 2% per annum on a straight line basis;
Plant and equipment   – 20% per annum on a straight line basis; and
Motor vehicles   – 20% per annum on a straight line basis.

14. The current tax estimated to be payable on profits for the year ended 31 December 2011, after taking account of all adjustments, is estimated to be €/£800,000.

Task 2.1

The book-keeper has asked for your assistance with the preparation of Holinwall's state-ment of comprehensive income for the year ended 31 December 2011, together with the statement of financial position as at that date.

Note: Students should also be able to prepare a memorandum and/or report for either internal or external stakeholders that clearly explains each of the adjustments made to the draft trial balance. This should be written in a style appropriate for the intended audience and, inter alia, explain the rationale/justification for the adjustment/ non-adjustment together with the accounting standard relied upon (where appropriate).

Task 2.2

Required Study

Connolly: Chapter 23 – Earnings Per Share

Self-test Questions
1. To what companies does IAS 33 apply?
2. Define earnings per share.
3. Following a rights issue what is the fraction by which the EPS for the corresponding previous period should be multiplied?
4. Summarise the disclosure requirements of IAS 33.

Calculate the basic earnings per share for Holinwall for the year ended 31 December 2011.

And finally:

Just before you leave for a well-earned skiing holiday, Catherine Clarke presents you with a list of questions that she believes would be useful for you to attempt before progressing to Session Three:

Connolly: **Chapter 7** – Borrowing Costs
Review Question 7.1
Challenging Question 7.1

Connolly: **Chapter 8** – Leases
Review Questions 8.1–8.4
Challenging Questions 8.1 and 8.2

Connolly: **Chapter 9** – Intangible Assets
Review Questions 9.1 and 9.2
Challenging Questions 9.1 and 9.2

Connolly: **Chapter 10** – Impairment
Review Questions 10.1 and 10.2
Challenging Questions 10.1 and 10.2

Connolly: **Chapter 11** – Inventories
        Review Questions 11.1 and 11.2
        Challenging Questions 11.1 and 11.2

Connolly: **Chapter 14** – Provisions, Contingent Liabilities and Contingent Assets
        Review Questions 14.1–14.4
        Challenging Questions 14.1–14.4

Connolly: **Chapter 16** – Accounting for Government Grants and Disclosure of Government Assistance
        Review Questions 16.1 and 16.2
        Challenging Questions 16.1–16.3

Connolly: **Chapter 20** – Non-Current Assets Held for Sale and Discontinued Operations
        Review Question 20.1
        Challenging Questions 20.1 and 20.2

Connolly: **Chapter 22** – Related Party Disclosures
        Review Questions 22.1–22.16
        Challenging Questions 22.1–22.3

Connolly: **Chapter 23** – Earnings Per Share
        Review Questions 23.1–23.3
        Challenging Questions 23.1–23.3

Connolly: **Chapter 31** – Foreign Currency Transactions and Translation of Foreign Operations
        Review Question 31.1
        Challenging Question 31.1

She strongly stresses to you the importance of attempting these questions under examination conditions in the appropriate time.

Congratulations, you have now finished Session Two. Relax, take a (short) break and when you are ready, begin Session Three which focuses on the analysis and interpretation of financial statements.

ANALYSIS AND INTERPRETATION OF FINANCIAL STATEMENTS

On successful completion of this session, you should be able to:

- calculate the main ratios and statistics commonly used in interpreting financial statements; and
- produce internal and external reports for a variety of users that analyse results over time or between activities.

Required Study

Connolly: Chapter 35 – Analysis and Interpretation of Financial Information

Self-test Questions
1. When is ratio analysis used?
2. What are the limitations of ratio analysis?
3. Name the main categories of ratio analysis.
4. How do you treat one-time charges in ratio analysis?
5. Who are the primary users of ratio analysis?

Competency Level: Integration

Getting Started

Ratio analysis can be used to assess the performance of a business. It can be used to analyse profitability, liquidity, solvency and returns to shareholders.

Task 3.1

Obtain a copy of the annual reports and financial statements for two companies operating in similar industries (for example: Easyjet plc and Ryanair Holdings plc; Sainsburys plc and Tesco plc; Orange plc and Vodafone Group plc; or perhaps two client companies).

Using the annual reports and financial statements referred to above, prepare a report using the CORE[3] integrated financial appraisal framework to analyse and compare the performance of the two chosen companies. Your analysis should: compare the narrative sections of the two annual reports; include the calculation of appropriate financial ratios; highlight any differences in key accounting policies; and consider any significant post publication events.

Meeting 3.1

While standing photocopying a colleague's notes from the lectures you missed while skiing, and contemplating your aching limbs and forthcoming credit card bill, John Keane unexpectedly asks you to accompany him to a meeting with the directors of Holinwall. After hurriedly transferring all the rubbish from the inside of your car to the boot, including the many pads of office paper, you collect him from the front door of the office, hoping that there is enough petrol in the car.

At the meeting, you discover that the directors of Holinwall are investigating the possibility of investing in Teckno Limited (Teckno), a small, but specialised, Irish retail company selling electronic equipment and parts. The statements of comprehensive income for the year ended 31 December 2010 and 2011, together with the statements of financial position as at those dates, are presented below.

Teckno
Statement of Comprehensive Income for the Year Ended 31 December

	2011	2010
	€/£	€/£
Revenue	929,812	934,276
Cost of sales	(504,665)	(519,271)
Gross profit	425,147	415,005
Investment income	7,149	7,831
Net operating expenses (including material operating items*)	(353,825)	(334,247)
	78,471	88,589
Loss on disposal of subsidiary undertaking**	(852)	–
	77,619	88,589
Finance costs	(9,781)	(11,329)
Profit before taxation	67,838	77,260

---

[3]Moon, P. and Bates, K. (1993), 'Core analysis in strategic perormance apprasial', *Management Accounting research,* Vol. 4, pp 139 - 152.

Income tax expense	(22,376)	(27,492)
Profit for the year	45,462	49,768
Ordinary dividends paid***	(23,074)	(17,040)
Retained earnings for the year	22,388	32,728

Note:
* IAS 1 *Presentation of Financial Statements* requires material items of income and expense to be disclosed separately (see **Connolly,** Chapter 2). Material items, which are also commonly referred to as 'exceptional items', are items which, in management's judgement, need to be disclosed by virtue of their size or incidence in order for the user to obtain a proper understanding of the financial information.
**Shown separately on the face of the statement of comprehensive income for ease of analysis.
***Should be included in the statement of changes in equity; disclosed here for ease of analysis (see **Connolly,** Chapter 2) .

Teckno
Statement of Financial Position as at 31 December

	2011	2010
	€/£	€/£
ASSETS		
Non-current Assets		
Land, property, plant and equipment	155,791	198,709
Development costs	186,347	207,414
	342,138	406,123
Current Assets		
Inventory	128,084	147,906
Trade receivables	11,481	16,889
Current asset investments	210,478	170,478
Bank and cash	41,258	37,251
	733,439	778,647
EQUITY AND LIABILITIES		
Capital and Reserves		
€/£1 ordinary shares	11,899	11,752
Share premium account	157,129	151,836
Capital redemption reserve	706	706
Retained earnings	183,269	160,881
	353,003	325,175

Non-current Liabilities

Borrowings	84,821	95,898
Other liabilities	7,559	14,257
Provisions	16,591	19,748
Current Liabilities		
Borrowings	170,478	172,478
Trade payables	100,987	151,091
	733,439	778,647

Task 3.2

While returning to the office with a nervous eye on the petrol gauge, John Keane asks you to:

(a) Calculate and explain the following ratios for Teckno in 2010 and 2011: (i) Return on capital employed (ROCE); (ii) Gross profit margin; (iii) Net profit margin; (iv) Current ratio; (v) Gearing ratio; and (vi) Inventory turnover (days).
(b) Using the ratios calculated in (a), prepare a brief report commenting on the performance of Teckno between 2010 and 2011.

Task 3.3

(a) Due to the competitive nature of the industry and the current economic climate, the directors of Holinwall are conscious of the need to reduce costs where possible. After conducting various sensitivity analyses, the directors of Holinwall believe that the company's return on capital employed and profit margins could be improved if the company made a number of current salaried employees redundant and replaced them with lower paid contract staff. Moreover, in addition to the likely improvement in Holinwall's price earnings ratio, the policy should have a favourable impact on directors' bonuses. However, the directors are also conscious of the growing need for the company to demonstrate that it is socially responsible.
(b) Prepare a briefing note for the attention of John Keane that discusses the ethical issues associated with Holinwall implementing a policy that utilises lower paid contract staff rather than higher paid salaried employees.

And finally:

On the day the office closes for the Easter holidays, Catherine Clarke presents you with more questions that she believes would be useful for you to attempt before progressing to Session Four:

Connolly: **Chapter 35** – Analysis and Interpretation of Financial Information
Review Questions 35.1–35.6
Challenging Questions 35.1–35.6

She strongly stresses to you the importance of attempting these questions under examination conditions in the appropriate time. In addition, she also advises you to review the ethical issues examined in Question 1 of the Summer 2009, Summer 2010 and Autumn 2010 CAP 2 Financial Reporting examination papers.

Congratulations, you have now finished Session Three. Relax, take a (short) break and when you are ready, begin Session Four which focuses on the preparation of consolidated financial statements.

SESSION FOUR

PREPARATION OF CONSOLIDATED FINANCIAL STATEMENTS

At the end of this session you should be able to:

- identify and address consolidated accounting issues; and
- prepare a consolidated statement of comprehensive income, statement of financial position and statement of cash flows.

Competency Level: Integration.

Meeting 4.1

Connolly: Chapter 26 – Business Combinations and Consolidated Financial Statements

Self-test Questions
1. Summarise the main features of IFRS 10.
2. Summarise the main features of IFRS 3.
3. Explain how goodwill should be calculated in accordance with IFRS 3.
4. Describe the two ways in which non-controlling interests may be calculated under IFRS 3.

Connolly: Chapter 29 – Associates

Self-test Questions
1. Explain the terms associate and significant influence.
2. Explain the equity method of accounting and how it differs from the consolidation approach used for subsidiaries.

It is mid-November 2012 (time flies when you are having fun.. or just working all the time).

John Keane met with the directors of Holinwall over lunch to discuss the preparation and audit of the company's 2012 consolidated financial statements. Shortly afterwards, he called you into his office and handed you a post-it containing some notes that he had taken during the lunch.

Task 4.1

Prepare a letter, for approval by John Keane, addressed to the directors of Holinwall explaining the crucial difference between the approach taken when consolidating subsidiary company results and incorporating the results of an associate company as far as the statement of financial position and statement of comprehensive income are concerned.

Meeting 4.2

Required Study

Connolly: Chapter 27 – Consolidated Statement of Financial Position

Self-test Questions
1. Explain how the investment in a subsidiary is reported in the parent's own financial statements.
2. Explain the difference between pre-acquisition and post-acquisition profits of a subsidiary.
3. Explain how inter-company balances should be treated in the consolidated statement of financial position.
4. Explain how negative goodwill may arise and its accounting treatment.
5. Discuss briefly the main reasons for the preparation of consolidated financial statements.

Connolly: Chapter 28 – Consolidated Statement of Comprehensive Income

Self-test Questions
1. List and explain six of the most common adjustments typically encountered in the preparation of a consolidated statement of comprehensive income.
2. Explain how the following issues should be dealt with when preparing a consolidated statement of comprehensive income:
   - Revaluation of assets;
   - Acquisition of a subsidiary during the accounting period;
   - Opening unrealised inventory profit;
   - Pre-acquisition reserves; and
   - Intergroup transfer of tangible non-current assets.

Connolly: Chapter 33 – Statement of Cash Flows – Consolidated

John Keane has asked for your assistance in preparing the consolidated financial statements of Holinwall for the year ended 31 December 2012.

The draft statements of comprehensive income of Holinwall and Teckno for the year ended 31 December 2012 and their statements of financial position as at 31 December 2012 are presented below. The statement of comprehensive income for the year ended 31 December 2011 and statement of financial position as at 31 December 2011 of Holinwall are also provided below.

Draft Statement of Comprehensive Income for the Year Ended 31 December

Holinwall 2011 €/£		Holinwall 2012 €/£	Teckno 2012 €/£
20,000,000	Revenue	26,000,000	950,000
(9,000,000)	Cost of sales	(12,500,000)	(500,000)
11,000,000	Gross profit	13,500,000	450,000
(6,575,307)	Net operating expenses	(8,743,943)	(350,000)
4,424,693	Operating profit	4,756,057	100,000
(74,250)	Finance cost	(82,000)	–
4,350,443	Profit before tax	4,674,057	100,000
(800,000)	Income tax expense	(850,000)	(40,000)
3,550,443	Profit after tax	3,824,057	60,000

Draft Statement of Financial Position as at 31 December

Holinwall 2011 €/£		Holinwall 2012 €/£	Teckno 2012 €/£
	ASSETS		
	Non-current Assets		
4,473,400	Land, property, plant, equipment and motor vehicles	7,000,000	180,000
900,000	Development costs	1,000,000	190,000
5,373,400		8,000,000	370,000

Holinwall 2011 €/£		Holinwall 2012 €/£	Teckno 2012 €/£
	Current Assets		
1,000,000	Inventory	1,850,000	130,000
1,200,000	Trade receivables	1,300,000	12,000
260,000	Other receivables and prepayments	280,000	–
–	Current account with Teckno	50,000	–
–	Current asset investments	–	240,000
180,000	Bank and cash	200,000	22,003
8,013,400		11,680,000	774,003
	EQUITY AND LIABILITIES		
	Capital and Reserves		
600,000	€/£1 ordinary shares	600,000	11,899
150,000	Share premium	150,000	157,129
–	Capital redemption reserve	–	706
3,550,443	Retained earnings	7,374,500	243,269
4,300,443		8,124,500	413,003
	Non-current Liabilities		
50,000	€/£2 Cumulative redeemable preference shares	50,000	–
750,000	Bank borrowings	500,000	80,000
13,500	Finance lease	58,250	–
–	Other liabilities	–	6,000
250,000	Provisions	200,000	15,000
	Current Liabilities		
250,000	Bank borrowings	250,000	160,000
1,240,000	Trade payables	1,300,000	90,000
272,207	Other payables and accruals	260,000	–
2,000	Preference dividends	2,000	–
800,000	Taxation	850,000	–
5,250	Finance lease	45,250	–

80,000	Deferred income	40,000	–
-	Current account with Holinwall	-	10,000
8,013,400		11,680,000	774,003

Additional Information:

1. Holinwall acquired 90% of the €/£ ordinary shares of Teckno on 1 January 2012, but has not yet recorded the investment in its books and records. The statement of financial position of Teckno at 1 January 2012 showed the following:

	€/£
Land, property, plant, equipment and motor vehicles	155,791
Development costs	186,347
Inventory	128,084
Trade receivables	11,481
Current asset investments	210,478
Bank and cash	41,258
	733,439
€/£1 ordinary shares	11,899
Share premium account	157,129
Capital redemption reserve	706
Retained earnings	183,269
	353,003
Non-current Liabilities	
Borrowings	84,821
Other liabilities	7,559
Provisions	16,591
Current Liabilities	
Borrowings	170,478
Trade payables	100,987
	733,439

The purchase consideration comprised of the issue of 300,000 €/£1 ordinary shares in Holinwall on 1 January 2012 and a cash payment of €/£1 million on 31 December 2014 if Teckno achieves defined profit targets. All indications are that Teckno will meet the defined profit targets. The market value of Holinwall's shares on 1 January 2012 was €/£1.98 per share, and the company could borrow at a fixed rate of 10% per annum for a three-year loan on this date.

While Holinwall did not incur any additional accountancy fees in connection with the acquisition of Teckno, it is estimated that the cost of Holinwall's directors time amounted to €/£40,000. This is included within operating expenses in the statement of comprehensive income of Holinwall for the year ended 31 December 2011, along with a €/£5,000 underwriting fee related to the issue of shares for Teckno.

In arriving at the consideration for the shares in Teckno, land was revalued upwards by €/£800,000 and trade receivables of €/£4,993 were deemed irrecoverable. No adjustment has been made in the books of Teckno in respect of these revaluations. The directors wish to give effect to the revaluations in the consolidated financial statements for the year ended 31 December 2012.

With respect to the measurement of non-controlling interests at the date of acquisition, the proportionate share method equated to the fair value method. The directors of Holinwall estimate that the goodwill arising on the acquisition of Teckno was impaired by €/£10,000 at 31 December 2012.

2. On 30 December 2012, Teckno sent a cheque for €/£40,000 to Holinwall that was not received until 3 January 2013.

3. During the year ended 31 December 2012, Holinwall sold raw materials to Teckno at an invoice price of €/£100,000. The raw materials were invoiced at cost plus 25%. One half of these raw materials was still in Teckno's inventory at 31 December 2012.

4. Additions to the land, property, plant, equipment and motor vehicles of Holinwall during 2012 include items purchased under finance lease contracts which would have cost €/£100,000 if purchased outright. Also, interest paid during the year of €/£10,000, relating to the construction of a warehouse, was capitalised by Holinwall.

Depreciation charged in arriving at operating profit in the statement of comprehensive income of Holinwall and Teckno for the year ended 31 December 2012 amounted to €/£380,000 and €/£30,000 respectively.

The operating expenses of Holinwall for the year ended 31 December 2012 includes a loss on the disposal of plant and equipment of €/£120,000. Proceeds of €/£10,000 were received.

5. Finance costs shown in the statement of comprehensive income of Holinwall for the years ended 31 December 2011 and 2012 comprise:

	2012 €/£	2011 €/£
Bank borrowings	65,000	70,000
Finance lease rentals	15,000	2,250
Preference dividend	2,000	2,000
	82,000	74,250

Based upon the substance of the contractual arrangement and the definition of a financial liability contained in IAS 32 *Financial Instruments: Presentation*, the directors of Holinwall have classified the 5% €/£2 cumulative redeemable preference shares as a financial liability. As a result, the preference shares are shown within non-current liabilities and the preference dividend is included as a component of finance costs.

Task 4.2

(a) Prepare the consolidated statement of comprehensive income of Holinwall for the year ended 31 December 2012 and the consolidated statement of financial position as at that date.

(A statement of how profit has been dealt with in the holding company, notes to the financial statements and comparative figures are NOT required. Your solution may be presented in the form of a working/consolidation schedule.)

(b) Prepare the consolidated statement of cash flows of Holinwall for the year ended 31 December 2012 in accordance with IAS 7 *Statement of Cash Flows*.

(Notes to the consolidated statement of cash flows are NOT required.)

Note:
1. All workings should be shown and assumptions should be clearly stated.
2. The following annuity table should be used where appropriate.

Period	10%
1	0.909
2	0.826
3	0.751

Required Study

Connolly: Chapter 23 – Earnings Per Share

Self-test Questions
1. To what companies does IAS 33 apply?
2. Define basic and diluted EPS.
3. Following a rights issue what is the fraction by which the EPS for the corresponding previous period should be multiplied?
4. Summarise the disclosure requirements of IAS 33.

Task 4.3

Calculate the basic earnings per share for Holinwall Group for the year ended 31 December 2012 in accordance with IAS 33 *Earnings per Share*.

And finally:

Just before you leave for your study leave, Catherine Clarke presents you with a selection of questions that she believes would be useful to attempt:

Connolly: Chapter 23 – Earnings Per Share
Review Questions 23.1–23.3
Challenging Questions 23.1–23.3

Connolly: Chapter 26 – Business Combinations and Consolidated Financial Statements
Review Question 26.1
Challenging Questions 26.1 and 26.2

Connolly: Chapter 27 – Consolidated Statement of Financial Position
Review Questions 27.1–27.3
Challenging Questions 27.1–27.4

Connolly: Chapter 28 – Consolidated Statement of Comprehensive Income
Review Questions 28.1–28.6
Challenging Questions 28.1–28.3

Connolly: Chapter 29 – Associates
Review Questions 29.1–29.3
Challenging Questions 29.1–29.5

Connolly: Chapter 33 – Statement of Cash Flows – Consolidated
Review Questions 33.1 and 33.2
Challenging Questions 33.1–33.3

She strongly stresses to you the importance of attempting these questions under examination conditions in the appropriate time.

Congratulations, you have now finished Session Four. Relax, take a (short) break and, when you are ready, begin again!

SUGGESTED SOLUTIONS
TO TASKS

SESSION ONE

SUGGESTED SOLUTIONS

Task 1.1

Letter addressed to Directors of Holinwall.

Key Points:

- Ordinary shares – these are the most common type of shares and generally carry voting rights in proportion to the number of shares held. An ordinary dividend does not have to be declared/approved each year, and the amount of ordinary dividend received will be based upon the number of ordinary shares held;
- Preference shares – these usually carry a specific rate of return (e.g. 5%) and require a payment each year for every share held. For example, with respect to Holinwall, 10 c/p each year for each preference share held (5% x €/£2). Some preference shares may be cumulative; therefore if the company does not make sufficient profit in any one year to pay the amount due to preference shareholders, it carries forward to the following year and accumulates until paid. Preference shares may also be redeemable, giving the company the right to repay the capital to the preference shareholders at a predetermined future date;
- Both ordinary shares and preference shares can be issued at a value greater than their nominal value i.e. issued at a premium.

In addition to the points above, it is necessary to bear in mind the issue of financial instruments when considering shares. A financial instrument is a contract that gives rise to a financial asset of one entity and a financial liability or equity instrument of another entity (see Connolly, Chapter 25). Once an item has been identified as a financial instrument, the next decision is whether to classify it as either a financial liability or an equity instrument. Consistent with the *Conceptual Framework for Financial Reporting 2010* (see Connolly, Chapter 1), a financial instrument should be classified as either an equity instrument or a financial liability according to the substance of the contract, not its legal form. IAS 32 *Financial Instruments: Presentation* states that the enterprise must make this decision at the time the instrument is initially recognised. The classification cannot be subsequently changed based on changed circumstances.

IAS 32 states that a financial instrument is an equity instrument only if:
- the instrument includes no contractual obligation to deliver cash or another financial asset to another entity; and
- if the instrument will or may be settled in the issuer's own equity instruments, it is either:
  - a non-derivative that includes no contractual obligation for the issuer to deliver a variable number of its own equity instruments; or
  - a derivative that will be settled only by the issuer exchanging a fixed amount of cash or another financial asset for a fixed number of its own equity instruments.

The key issue in determining whether an instrument is a liability is the existence of a contractual obligation for the issuer to deliver cash or another financial asset. This is in contrast to an equity instrument where any payment is at the discretion of the issuer. (**Examples 25.2** and **25.3** in Connolly, Chapter 25, illustrate the application of this in practice.)

In broad terms, if an enterprise issues preference shares that pay a fixed rate of dividend and that have a mandatory redemption feature (e.g. must be repaid on a specified date and amount in the future), the substance is that they are a contractual obligation to deliver cash and, therefore, should be recognised as a liability. Where preference shares are issued at a premium and the shares are recognised as a liability then the premium forms part of the liability. Dividends on the shares that are recognised as a liability should be disclosed as a separate component of finance costs for the year.

Task 1.2

Letter addressed to directors of Holinwall.

Key Points:

1. All shares are issued at par

   600,000 €/£1 ordinary shares; and
   100,000 5% €/£2 preference shares, resulting in a preference dividend of €/£10,000.
2. The ordinary shares are issued at a premium of 25 c/p and the preference shares at a premium of 50 c/p.

600,000 €/£1 ordinary shares at €/£1.25	=	€/£750,000; and
20,000 5% €/£2 preference shares at €/£2.50	=	€/£50,000, resulting in a preference dividend of €/£2,000.

(Note: The dividend paid is based upon the nominal value of the share.)

Task 1.3

Letter addressed to directors of Holinwall.

Key Points:

(a) In most (large) companies, it is not possible for all shareholders to be involved in the management of the company, nor do most wish to be involved. Instead they appoint directors to act on their behalf. This separation of ownership from day-to-day control creates the need for directors to be accountable for their stewardship of the company's assets.

Benefits and Beneficiaries:

- Inform and protect shareholders – if shareholders do not receive information about the performance and position of the company, they will have problems in appraising their investment. Under these circumstances, they would probably be reluctant to invest and this, in turn, would affect the functioning of the private sector. Any society with a significant private sector needs to encourage equity investment;
- Inform and protect suppliers of labour, goods, services and finance – individuals and organisations would be reluctant to engage in commercial relationships, such as supplying goods or lending money, where a company does not provide information about its financial health. The fact that a company has limited liability increases the risks involved in dealing with the company. An unwillingness to engage in commercial relationships with limited companies will affect the functioning of the private sector; and
- Inform and protect society – some companies exercise enormous power and influence in society, particularly geographically on a local basis. For example, a particular company may be a dominant employer and purchaser of commercial goods and services in a particular town or city. Legislators have tended to take the view that society has the right to information about the company and its activities.

(b) Accounting can never really be said to be 'correct' or 'accurate' as these words imply that there is a precise value that any asset, claim, revenue or expense could have. This is simply not true in many, if not most, cases. For example, the annual depreciation expense is based on judgements about the future, concerning the estimated useful economic life and residual value of the asset. If all relevant factors are taken into account and reasonable judgements are applied, it might be possible to achieve a fair representation of the amount of the cost or fair value of the asset that is consumed in a particular period. However, it is extremely unlikely that a precise figure for depreciation for a period could be achieved.

Task 1.4

E-mail addressed to Holinwall's book-keeper.

Key Points:

While the amount due to the dealership is €/£42,000, the transactions should be accounted for as follows:

Acquisition of car:

		€/£
New Audi TT	- Purchase price	40,000
Delivery charge	- Part of capital cost as necessary and integral	200
Alloy wheels	- Part of capital cost as necessary and integral	1,500

Sunroof	- Part of capital cost as necessary and integral	1,800
Number plates	- Part of capital cost as necessary and integral	150
Capitalise and depreciate[1.]		43,650

[1.] The part exchange value is not relevant in relation to the total cost of the new car, although it is relevant with respect to the calculation of the profit/loss on disposal.

		€/£
Petrol	- Charge to 2011 statement of comprehensive income in arriving at profit before tax	100
Road fund licence[2.]	- Charge to 2011 statement of comprehensive income	250
		350

[2.] Road fund licence could be prepaid depending on period/year end.

Disposal of van:

	€/£
Original cost	3,000
Accumulated depreciation[3.]	–
	3,000
Proceeds received	(2,000)
Loss on disposal	1,000

[3.] The Reliant Robin was acquired and disposed of in the same year. Although it is company policy to charge a full year's depreciation in the year of acquisition and none in the year of disposal, any depreciation can be ignored as the impact on the statement of comprehensive income will be same.

Recording the transactions:

		DR	CR
		€/£	€/£
DR	Motor vehicles	43,650	
DR	Statement of comprehensive income – administrative expenses	350	
DR	Motor vehicles disposal account	3,000	
DR	Statement of comprehensive income – administrative expenses (loss)	1,000	
CR	Bank		42,000

CR	Motor vehicles	3,000
CR	Disposal account	2,000
CR	Disposal account	1,000

- being acquisition of Audi TT and disposal of Reliant Robin.

Task 1.5

Key Points:

Despite the proliferation of accounting rules, some directors apply particular accounting policies or structure transactions in such a way as to portray a picture of financial health that is in line with what they would like users to see rather than what is a true and fair view of the company's financial position and performance.

Why?

- Get around restrictions (to report sufficient profit to enable a dividend to be paid);
- Avoid government action (tax on profits);
- Hide poor management decisions;
- Achieve sales and/or profit targets, thereby ensuring that performance bonuses are paid;
- Attract new share capital or loan capital by showing a healthy financial position; and/or
- Satisfy the demands of major investors concerning levels of return.

Methods:

- Overstating revenue (e.g. early recognition);
- Massaging expenses (especially those that rely on judgement of directors/particular accounting policies. For example, depreciation research and development, inventory valuation, bad debt provisions);
- Concealing bad news (e.g. by creating a separate entity to take over losses/liabilities); and/or
- Overstating assets (e.g. by revaluing assets using figures greater than market value, or capitalising costs that should be written off as an expense.

Task 1.6

Letter addressed to Holinwall's book-keeper.

Key Points:

(a)

- Non-current assets often increase in value due to circumstances outside a company's control. For example, land and property tend to increase in value in the same way that house prices usually do. Providing this information could be extremely relevant and important to users of the company's financial statements as the company could sell the assets and thus increase the net worth of the business;

- Companies are allowed to carry (all) non-current assets within a particular class at their revalued amount (see Connolly, Chapter 6 and IAS 16 *Property, Plant and Equipment*); and
- Departing from the historical costing accounting convention does have accounting implications in terms of how the changes in value are accounted for. It is important to distinguish between non-current assets dealt with under IAS 16 and those accounted for under IAS 40 *Investment Property* (see Connolly, Chapter 5).

(b)

Points might include:

The practice of giving and receiving gifts has always been a very fine ethical question. Ideally gifts should not be seen as an inducement to promote business in a manner that is not open and honest.

Although gifts might be a sign of goodwill and respect, it is important to bear in mind:
- the scale of the gifts – small, low value items are unlikely to be perceived as inducement and therefore not considered unethical (e.g. diaries, low cost pens etc.);
- the payment of 'bribes' to encourage business is unacceptable in the view of most people, although it could be common practice in some countries and industries; and
- organisations should have a precise code for dealing with both giving and receiving gifts, including where government officials are involved.

Social, environmental and ethical reporting is experiencing an increasing role and prominence. The professional accountancy bodies, including Chartered Accountants Ireland, have issued codes of professional conduct, with the key themes being: integrity; objectivity; professional competence; and confidentiality.

Session Two

SUGGESTED SOLUTIONS

Task 2.1

Holinwall
Statement of Comprehensive Income for the Year Ended 31 December 2011

	€/£	€/£
Revenue		20,000,000
Cost of Sales:		
Opening inventory		-
Purchases	8,000,000	
Production overheads	2,000,000	
Closing inventory	(1,000,000)	(9,000,000)
Gross profit		11,000,000
Administrative expenses	5,395,307	
Selling and distribution costs	1,180,000	(6,575,307)
		4,424,693
Finance costs		(74,250)
		4,350,443
Income tax expense		(800,000)
		3,550,443

Holinwall
Statement of Financial Position as at 31 December 2011

	€/£	€/£
ASSETS		
Non-current Assets		
Land		1,000,000
Property – cost	2,680,000	
Property – accumulated depreciation	(53,600)	2,626,400
Plant and equipment – cost	942,500	
Plant and equipment – accumulated depreciation	(191,500)	751,000
Motor vehicles – cost	120,000	
Motor vehicles – accumulated depreciation	(24,000)	96,000
Development costs		900,000
		5,373,400
Current Assets		
Inventory		1,000,000
Trade receivables		1,200,000
Other receivables and prepayments		260,000
Bank and cash		180,000
		8,013,400
EQUITY AND LIABILITIES		
Capital and Reserves		
€/£1 ordinary shares		600,000
Share premium		150,000
Retained earnings		3,550,443
		4,300,443

Non-current Liabilities

5% €/£2 Cumulative redeemable preference shares	50,000
Bank borrowings	750,000
Finance lease	13,500
Provisions	250,000

Current Liabilities

Bank borrowings	250,000
Trade payables	1,240,000
Other payables and accruals	272,207
Preference dividends	2,000
Taxation	800,000
Finance lease	5,250
Deferred income	80,000
	8,013,400

Holinwall
Draft Trial Balance as at 31 December 2011

	PER DRAFT TB DR €/£	PER DRAFT TB CR €/£	ADJUSTMENTS DR €/£	ADJUSTMENTS CR €/£	FINAL DR €/£	FINAL CR €/£
Revenue		20,000,000				20,000,000
Purchases of raw materials	8,000,000		8,000,000			
Production overheads (excluding direct cost of raw materials)	2,000,000		2,000,000			
Administrative expenses	2,500,000		(w13) 159,000		5,395,307	
Selling and distribution costs	1,100,000		(w10) 80,000		1,180,000	
Finance costs	250,000		(w4) 2,250 (w11) 2,000	(w3a) 180,000	74,250	
€/£1 ordinary shares		600,000				600,000
Share premium – ordinary shares		150,000				150,000
5% €/£2 cumulative redeemable preference shares		40,000				40,000
Share premium – preference shares		10,000				10,000
Land – cost at 31 December 2011	1,000,000			1,000,000		
Property – cost at 31 December 2011	2,500,000		(w3a) 180,000		2,680,000	

Adjustments (ADJUSTMENTS DR €/£):

```
(w1)  275,000
(w3b)   3,600
(w4)    3,300
(w5)    1,207
(w5)    3,200
(w7) 2,100,000
(w7)  100,000
(w9)  250,000
(w13)  159,000
(w10)   80,000
(w4)    2,250
(w11)   2,000
```

Holinwall
Draft Trial Balance as at 31 December 2011 *(Cont.)*

	PER DRAFT TB		ADJUSTMENTS		FINAL	
	DR €/£	CR €/£	DR €/£	CR €/£	DR €/£	CR €/£
Property – accumulated depreciation at 31 December 2011		–		(w3b) 3,600 (w13) 50,000		53,600
Plant and equipment – cost at 31 December 2011	700,000		(w4) 16,500 (w5) 16,000 (w7) 500,000	(w1) 275,000 (w5) 15,000	942,500	
Plant and equipment – accumulated depreciation at 31 December 2011		–		(w4) 3,300 (w5) 3,200 (w7) 100,000 (w13) 85,000		191,500
Motor vehicles – cost at 31 December 2011	120,000				120,000	
Motor vehicles – accumulated depreciation at 31 December 2011		–		(w13) 24,000		24,000
Research expenditure	3,500,000			(w7) 2,100,000 (w7) 500,000	900,000	
Trade receivables	1,200,000				1,200,000	
Other receivables and prepayments	260,000				260,000	
Bank and cash	180,000				180,000	
Trade payables		1,240,000				1,240,000
Other payables and accruals		270,000	(w5) 15,000	(w5) 16,000 (w5) 1,207		272,207
Bank borrowings – current		250,000				250,000

Holinwall
Draft Trial Balance as at 31 December 2011 *(Cont.)*

	PER DRAFT TB		ADJUSTMENTS		FINAL	
	DR	CR	DR	CR	DR	CR
	€/£	€/£	€/£	€/£	€/£	€/£
Bank borrowings – non-current	-	750,000				750,000
Current tax – statement of comprehensive income	-	-	(w14) 800,000		800,000	
Current tax – statement of financial position	-	-		(w14) 800,000		800,000
Proposed dividends – preference shares	-	-		(w11) 2,000		2,000
HP agreement – non-current liabilities	-	-	(w4) 6,000 (w4) 3,750 (w4) 5,250	(w4) 22,500 (w4) 2,250 (w4) 3,750		13,500
HP agreement – current liabilities	-	-		(w4) 5,250		5,250
Deferred income	-	-		(w10) 80,000		80,000
Provision for liabilities and charges	-	-		(w9) 250,000		250,000
Inventory – cost of sales	-	-		(w8a) 800,000 (w8b) 200,000		1,000,000
Inventory – statement of financial position	-	-	(w8a) 800,000 (w8b) 200,000		1,000,000	
	23,310,000	23,310,000			25,732,057	25,732,057

Workings:

1. Impairment review

In accordance with IAS 36 *Impairment of Assets* (see Connolly, Chapter 10), Holinwall must account for all impairments in the value of property, plant and equipment whether temporary or permanent.

	€/£
Net Realisable Value of Assets in Cash Generating Unit:	
Gross market value of plant and equipment	250,000
Less selling costs	(25,000)
	225,000

	€/£
Net Present Value of Future Cash Flows in Cash Generating Unit:	
Future cash flows €/£30,000 – €/£4,000 = €/£26,000 for 8 years @ 5.747 (8%)	149,422

	€/£
Net Book Value of Assets in Cash generating Unit:	
Direct book value of plant and equipment	400,000
Head office assets	100,000
	500,000

	€/£
Therefore impairment:	
NBV	500,000
NRV	(225,000)
	275,000

		DR €/£	CR €/£
DR	SCI – administrative expenses*	275,000	
CR	Plant and equipment		275,000

- Being impairment of plant and equipment.

* The impairment has been charged to administrative expenses on the basis that related depreciation would normally be charged to administrative expenses; the impairment could also be charged to cost of sales or selling and distribution costs.

2. Compulsory purchase order on land

There is only a probable sale and gain of €/£250,000 i.e. not certain. Therefore, in accordance with IAS 37 *Provisions, Contingent Liabilities and Contingent Assets* (see Connolly, Chapter 14) this represents a contingent gain. While it should not be recognised in the 2011 financial statements, it should be disclosed by way of note.

(Note: As indicated above, it is assumed that the sale is only probable i.e. not certain, and consequently no adjustment is required to the 2011 financial statements. IFRS 5 *Non-current Assets Held for Sale and Discontinued Operations* (see Connolly: Chapter 20) states that an entity must classify a non-current asset as held for sale if its carrying amount will be recovered principally through a sale transaction rather than through continuing use. This means that the asset must be available for immediate sale in its present condition and the sale must be highly probable. If this view is taken, then IFRS 5 should be applied.)

3. Capitalisation of the finance costs associated with the extension

Borrowings costs are 'traditionally' recognised as an expense when incurred. Indeed, the previous version of IAS 23 *Borrowing Costs* (which was in force until 1 January 2011) required that borrowing costs be normally recognised as an expense in the period incurred. Although, as an alternative, the previous version of IAS 23 allowed borrowing costs that were directly attributable to the acquisition, construction or production of a qualifying asset to be capitalised as part of the cost of that asset. In contrast, the revised IAS 23 (effective for accounting periods beginning on or after 1 January 2011) requires that qualifying borrowing costs *must* be capitalised (see Connolly, Chapter 7). Borrowing costs *must* be capitalised as part of the cost of an asset when:

*   is probable that the costs will result in future economic benefits and the costs can be reliably measured; and
*   they are directly attributable if they would have been avoided if the asset was not bought, constructed or produced.

Capitalisation should commence when expenditure on the asset and borrowing costs are being incurred, and must cease when substantially all the activities necessary to prepare the asset for sale or use are complete. Capitalisation should cease when substantially all the activities necessary to prepare the relevant asset for its intended use have been completed i.e. only interest incurred during the period of construction may be capitalised.

	€/£
€/£2,000,000 x 50% x 10%	100,000
€/£2,000,000 x 50% x 8%	80,000
	180,000

(a)		DR	CR
		€/£	€/£
DR	Property	180,000	
CR	Finance costs		180,000

- Being capitalisation of borrowing costs associated with extension of inventory storage facilities.

Property depreciation must also be increased accordingly.

		DR	CR
(b)		€/£	€/£
DR	SCI – administrative expenses	3,600	
	CR Property – accumulated depreciation (2%)		3,600

- Being additional depreciation due following capitalisation of borrowing costs associated with extension of inventory storage facilities.

4. Purchased of computer equipment

This is clearly a HP contract. The computer equipment is under the control of Holinwall.

	€/£
3 x €/£7,500 payments	22,500
Cost	16,500
Interest	6,000

			DR	CR
			€/£	€/£
DR		Plant and equipment	16,500	
DR		HP interest suspense	6,000	
	CR	Non-current liabilities – HP agreement		22,500
DR		SCI – administrative expenses – depreciation (20%)	3,300	
DR		SCI – finance costs*	2,250	
	CR	Plant and equipment – accumulated depreciation		3,300
	CR	HP suspense*		2,250
DR		Non-current liabilities – HP agreement	3,750	
	CR	HP interest suspense (net balance)		3,750
DR		Non-current liabilities – HP agreement	5,250	
	CR	Current liabilities – HP agreement (€/£7,500 - €/£2,250)		5,250

- Being capitalisation of computer equipment and recording of HP contract.
* Using sum of digits: [N(N + 1)/2] = 6. Therefore 3/6 x €/£6,000 x 9/12 = €/£2,250

5. Equipment purchased from Guyere using forward contract

			DR €/£	CR €/£
Correct Entry:				
DR		Plant and equipment (120,000 Swfr/7.5)	16,000	
	CR	Other payables and accruals		16,000
Reverse Incorrect Entry:				
DR		Other payables and accruals	15,000	
	CR	Plant and equipment (120,000 Swfr/8.0)		15,000
Reverse Translation Gain:				
DR		Administrative expenses*	1,207	
	CR	Other payables and accruals		1,207

* 120,000 Swfr/8.7 = €/£13,793 - €/£15000 = €/£1,207

Depreciation to be provided:

			DR €/£	CR €/£
DR		SCI – administrative expenses – depreciation (20%)	3,200	
	CR	Plant and equipment – accumulated depreciation (20%)		3,200

- Being depreciation due on equipment purchased from Guyere.

6. Acquisition of van under a four year lease

The total payments of €/£19,200 (48 x €/£400) are €/£700 greater than the purchase price. Normally 90% of the present value of the minimum lease payments must be covered and a large residual value is unlikely. However, as the van will only be four years old at the end of the lease term, some 'value' should revert to the lessor and therefore it is likely that there will be more than one user of the van. Consequently, the agreement appears to resemble an operating lease and no further adjustment is required.

7. Research expenditure

In the context of research expenditure (see Connolly, Chapter 9), IAS 38 *Intangible Assets* states that expenditure must meet the following criteria in order to be classified as development expenditure:

 (i) the expenditure must relate to a clearly defined project;
(ii) the expenditure must be separately identifiable;

(iii) the project must be technically feasible and commercially viable;

(iv) future revenue from the project must be sufficient to cover costs; and

 (v) there must be adequate resources to ensure that the project can be brought on stream.

For the purposes of the 2011 financial statements, the anticipated expenditure in 2010 can be ignored. With respect to the 2011 expenditure:

	€/£	
Feasibility study	500,000	Write off to SCI in 2011 in arriving at profit before tax
Initial research on service development	1,600,000	Write off to SCI in 2011 in arriving at profit before tax
Expenditure on the new service	900,000	Capitalise, and amortise 2012 – 2014
Plant and equipment	500,000	Capitalise, and depreciate from 2011
	3,500,000	

			DR	CR
			€/£	€/£
DR	SCI – administrative expenses		2,100,000	
	CR	Research expenditure		2,100,000

			DR	CR
DR	Plant and equipment		500,000	
DR	SCI – administrative expenses – depreciation		100,000	
	CR	Research expenditure		500,000
	CR	Plant and equipment – accumulated depreciation (20%)		100,000

– Being reclassification of research expenditure per draft trial balance.

8. Inventory and overhead expenditure

(a)			DR	CR
			€/£	€/£
DR	SFP – inventory		800,000	
	CR	SCI – cost of sales		800,000

- Being cost of inventory at 31 December 2011.

(b) Production overheads: €/£2,000,000 x 10% = €/£200,000

		DR €/£	CR €/£
DR	SFP – inventory	200,000	
CR	SCI – cost of sales		200,000

- Being inclusion of production overheads in inventory valuation at 31 December 2011.

9. Legal claim

It is probable that Holinwall will be found liable. Therefore, ignoring any liability insurance that the company may have, it is necessary to provide for the rectification costs in accordance with IAS 37 *Provisions, Contingent Liabilities and Contingent Assets* (see Connolly, Chapter 14).

		DR €/£	CR €/£
DR	SCI – administrative expenses	250,000	
CR	Non-current liabilities – provision		250,000

- Being provision for expected rectification costs.

10. Government grant

Under IAS 20 *Accounting for Government Grants and Disclosure of Government Assistance* (see Connolly, Chapter 14), the grant should be matched against the related expenditure. The grant should be released in proportion to the jobs created, with the balance shown as deferred income and released in future years to the statement of comprehensive income as the remaining jobs are created (expected to be 2012) (accruals concept).

		DR €/£	CR €/£
DR	SCI – selling and distribution costs	80,000	
CR	SFP – deferred income (8/20 x €/£200,000)		80,000

- Being deferred grant income in respect of jobs still to be created.

11. Dividends

Dividends are an appropriation and therefore should be taken through reserves and reflected in the Statement of Changes in Equity.

In accordance with IAS 10 *Events After the Reporting Period* (see Connolly, Chapter 15), proposed dividends are not accrued until approved by shareholders at the AGM. If a dividend is not declared and approved by the shareholders at the reporting date then no liability should be recognised (in respect of the previous period) as the dividends were not appropriately authorised at the reporting date and are therefore at the discretion of the entity. No present obligation exists while an entity still has discretion in relation to payment.

Therefore, the ordinary dividend cannot be accrued at 31 December 2011.

Please see suggested solution for *Task 1.1.* On the basis of the information provided, it appears that the preference shares pay a fixed rate of dividend (5% cumulative) and that they have a mandatory redemption feature, the substance is that they are a contractual obligation to deliver cash and therefore should be recognised as a liability. Where preference shares are issued at a premium and the shares are recognised as a liability then the premium forms part of the liability. Dividends on the shares that are recognised as a liability should be disclosed as a separate component of finance costs for the year. (This is discussed further in Connolly, Chapter 25 – see **Examples 25.2** and **25.3**).

Therefore, the preference dividend should be accrued at 31 December 2011 and disclosed as a separate component of finance costs.

		DR	CR
		€/£	€/£
DR	Finance costs (20,000 x €/£2 x 5%)	2,000	
CR	Current liabilities – proposed dividends		2,000

12. Related parties

Under IAS 24 *Related Party Disclosures* (see Connolly, Chapter 22), because of the close relationship between the directors, there is the chance that transactions between the two parties may not be conducted at arm's length. In order to ensure that organisations are open and transparent about their affairs with close parties, IAS 24 requires companies to disclose details of all material transactions even if on an arm's length basis and regardless of whether cash is involved. Therefore the legal fees of €/£80,000, cost of packaging materials of €/£275,000 and amount of €/£40,000 outstanding should be disclosed in the 2011 financial statements, together with a short narrative explaining the nature of the relationships. No adjustment is required to the 2011 financial statements.

13. Depreciation

Land	- nil;
Property	- 2% per annum on a straight line basis;
Plant and equipment	- 20% per annum on a straight line basis; and
Motor vehicles	- 20% per annum on a straight line basis.

	Land	Property	Plant and Equipment	Motor Vehicles
Depreciation policy	Nil	2% SL	20% SL	20% SL
	€/£	€/£	€/£	€/£
Per TB	1,000,000	2,500,000	700,000	120,000
Impairment (w1)			(275,000)	
			425,000	
Depreciation	–	50,000	85,000	24,000

			DR	CR
			€/£	€/£
DR		SCI – administrative expenses	159,000	
	CR	Accumulated depreciation – property		50,000
	CR	Accumulated depreciation – plant and equipment		85,000
	CR	Accumulated depreciation – motor vehicles		24,000

14. Current tax

			DR	CR
			€/£	€/£
DR		SCI – income tax expense	800,000	
	CR	Current liabilities – current taxation		800,000

Note: Students should also be able to prepare a memorandum and/or report for either internal or external stakeholders that clearly explains each of the adjustments made to the draft trial balance. This should be written in a style appropriate for the user and, inter alia, explain the rationale/justification for the adjustment/non-adjustment together with the accounting standard relied upon (where appropriate).

Task 2.2

Earnings:	€/£
Profit after tax	3,550,443

Number of Ordinary Shares:	
1 x 6/12	0.5
600,000 x 6/12	300,000
	300,000.5

EPS: $\dfrac{3,550,443}{300,000.5}$ = €/£11.83

SESSION THREE

SUGGESTED SOLUTIONS

Task 3.1

CORE is an acronym for: Context, Overview, Ratio analysis and Evaluation. The approach recommended by Moon and Bates (1993) addresses many of the problems associated with assessing company performance. Assessment may be done from a particular standpoint, such as that of a prospective investor, lender or supplier.

Context has two aspects – external and internal. This part of the analysis 'sets the scene'. It has two aspects, namely external profile and internal profile.

The external profile refers to: (1) the typical characteristics of the organisation being analysed; (2) its industrial/business sector, when considered under steady state conditions; and (3) changes in general market conditions during the period under review. The questions one should be asking to determine the external profile of an entity as regards categories (1) and (2) above are usually: what is it, what does it do, and what types of assets and liabilities are typical of an organisation in this sector? Expectations differ markedly for each different type of organisation and so one must interpret the indicators contingent on the type of organisation under scrutiny. As regards the industry/business sector in which the company operates, one needs to know whether there are any particular factors which affect performance. These are items peculiar to the industry, such as typical raw materials and whence they are purchased or the type of customer base. They are distinct from the changes in general market conditions referred to in (3) above. The latter are items outside an organisation's control which are imposed upon it and which it cannot influence. Such changes may be induced by the economic, political or legislative environment.

Internal profile refers to: (1) developments in the organisation's own strategic positioning within its particular business sector; and (2) critical success factors underlying its performance. Neither of these will be likely to be static and will respond to changes in the market place, technology, relevant statutory and quasi-statutory legislation. One needs to assess performance in the light of such changes. It could be that the corporate profile changes or certain business segments are discontinued. One must try to understand the scale of changes in circumstances like these to assess meaningfully a company's financial performance over a period of time and the likely sustainability of any competitive advantage obtained as a result of these changes – in other words, how critical success factors have developed over time.

To gain an overview of how the company has been performing, the accounts analyst looks at the financial statements of the company, and reads the Chairman's Report, the Directors' Report etc., and any other publicly available information. He/she looks at trends in sales, profits and asset and liability movements. No formal calculations are done at this stage, as the purpose is to get a 'feel' for how things are generally outside of any financial calculations. One should also be alert for items that distort figures, such as 'one-off' events like mergers, acquisitions, share issues, strikes, redundancies, major fires or fraud. Differences in accounting policy between one period and another are another cause of distortions. For example, if a company suddenly decided to include brand names as an asset on its statement of financial position, then assets would increase and ratios involving returns on capital, for example, would not be comparable with prior periods.

It is only after the context and overview have been established that Moon and Bates recommend calculating ratios, as they will now have a foundation on which to rest. The general advice is much as given above for ratios. Evaluation is the final stage in the Moon and Bates assessment process. Having gathered all this information, one must then interpret it. Here narrative explanations have their part to play, and the use of ratios in combination, to see whether a coherent picture is given – not only for the one year of one company, but for all other periods for which ratios have been calculated for that company, and for the competitors' ratios for all periods as well. Comparative features need to be highlighted to demonstrate how good or how bad the results are for any period in key strategic areas.

One should draw into this factors from the earlier parts of the analysis – context and overview – as well, and not just concentrate on the detailed explanation of ratios. One should endeavour to come to some conclusion as to the organisation's success in terms of what is known about its corporate strategy, etc. It may be that one is considering the financial results from a particular viewpoint, such as that of a prospective shareholder or lender. If so, the analysis will have been given a specific focus right from the start, and will need to be done from this point of view from the beginning. This harks back to the starting point mentioned above.

While the Moon and Bates approach does address many of the problems innate to company performance assessment, it cannot eliminate the problems inherent in ratio calculation itself. All ratio analysis is predicated on accounting figures, and given the underlying facility for manipulation and smoothing away distortions, no approach can eradicate this entirely.

Task 3.2

Part (a)

(i) Return on capital employed (ROCE)

ROCE is one of the most important ratios used to measure the performance of a business. The advantage of this ratio is that it relates profit to the size of the business. Profit is defined as net profit (or operating profit) before tax and interest. This is sometimes called earnings before interest and tax or 'EBIT'.

ROCE = profit before tax and interest ÷ long-term capital employed × 100.

For Teckno, the operating profit before tax and interest in 2011 was €/£71,322. Long-term capital employed was €/£445,383. Long term capital employed is shareholders' funds plus any long-term loans, i.e. €/£353,003 + €/£92, 380 (€/£84,821 + €/£7,559).

For 2011, ROCE = €/£71,322 ÷ €/£445,383 × 100 = 16.0%.

For 2010, ROCE = €/£80,758 ÷ €/£435,330 × 100 = 18.6%.

Obviously, a higher ROCE is better, and it has declined in 2011 compared with 2010. To determine how good the return is it would have to be compared with another similar business. The ROCE will vary according to the industry. However, if it is compared with what would be earned in a bank, say 5% in 2011, Teckno's return of 16% in 2011 is still favourable (although the risk of putting money into a business has to be taken into account).

(ii) Gross profit margin

The gross profit margin is also known as the 'mark-up'. This shows the gross profit made on sales turnover.

Gross profit margin = gross profit ÷ turnover × 100.

For Teckno in 2011 gross profit was €/£425,147 and turnover was €/£929,812.

For 2011, gross profit margin = €/£425,147 ÷ €/£929,812 × 100 = 45.7%.

For 2010, gross profit margin = €/£415,005 ÷ €/£934,276 × 100 = 44.4%.

Higher gross margins are preferable to lower ones, and it is encouraging that the gross profit margin has increased (albeit slightly) in 2011 compared with 2010. However, they vary significantly according to industry type. As a rule, the quicker the turnover of inventory is, the lower the gross margin. A retailer like Teckno, with a relatively fast inventory turnover, is likely to have a lower gross margin than (say) a car retailer or jeweller with a much slower inventory turnover. In this case, 45.7% seems to be a good margin.

(iii) Net profit margin

Net profit margin helps to measure how well a business controls its overheads. If the difference between the gross margin and the net margin is small, this suggests that overheads are low. This is because net profit equals gross profit less overheads.

Net profit margin = net profit before tax & interest ÷ turnover × 100.

For Teckno in 2011, net profit before tax and interest was €/£71,322 and turnover was €/£929,812.

For 2011, net profit margin = €/£71,322 ÷ €/£929,812 × 100 = 7.7%.

For 2010, net profit margin = €/£80,758 ÷ €/£934,276 × 100 = 8.6%.

Again, higher margins are naturally preferable to lower ones, and despite the increase in gross profit margin, the net profit margin has declined by 0.9% in 2011.

(iv) Current ratio

The current ratio is a liquidity ratio. It is used to assess whether a business has enough liquid assets to pay any immediate bills that arise. It focuses on current assets and current liabilities and is also known as the 'working capital ratio'.

Current ratio = current assets ÷ current liabilities

For Teckno in 2011, current assets were €/£391,301 and current liabilities were €/£271,465.

For 2011, current ratio = €/£391,301 ÷ €/£271,465 = 1.44.

For 2010, current ratio = €/£372,524 ÷ €/£323,569 = 1.15.

The current ratio has increased from 1.15 in 2010 to 1.44 in 2011. Generally, if a business has a current ratio of between 1.5 and 2.0, it is said to have enough liquid resources. If the ratio is below 1.5, it might be argued that a business does not have enough working capital. If the current ratio is above 2.0, money may be tied up unproductively. The current ratio for Teckno in 2011 was 1.44, just slightly under the 1.5 mark. Retailers often have very low current ratios, perhaps 1.0 or below. This is because they hold fast-selling inventory and generate cash from sales. Since Teckno is a retailer, and without having industry information, the current ratio of 1.44 in 2011 appears reasonable.

(v) Gearing ratio

The gearing ratio is used to assess the capital structure of a business. It compares the amount of share capital with loans. The gearing ratio can assess whether or not a business is burdened by its loans. This is because highly geared companies have to pay their interest even when trading becomes difficult.

Gearing ratio = fixed-cost capital ÷ long-term capital × 100.

Fixed-cost capital includes long-term loans from banks, certain preference shares and debentures. Long-term capital includes shareholders' funds and long-term loans. For Teckno in 2011, the fixed-cost or interest/dividend bearing debt, according to the statement of financial position, was loans of €/£92,380 (non-current liabilities). The value of shareholders' funds was €/£353,003.

For 2011, gearing ratio = €/£92,380 ÷ €/£445,383 × 100 = 20.7%.

For 2010, gearing ratio = €/£110,155 ÷ €/£435,330 × 100 = 25.3%.

When the gearing ratio is less than 50%, the company is said to be 'low geared'. This means that most of the capital is provided by the owners. If the ratio is greater than 50%, the company is highly geared. By contrast, this means that a much higher proportion of total capital is borrowed. With a gearing ratio of 25.3% in 2010 and 20.7% in 2011, Teckno was low geared and therefore not heavily in debt.

(vi) Inventory turnover

Inventory turnover measures how quickly a business uses or sells its inventory. One approach to inventory turnover is to calculate how many days it takes to sell the inventory.

Inventory turnover = inventory ÷ cost of sales × 365

For 2011, inventory turnover = €/£128,084 ÷ €/£504,665 × 365 = 93 days.

For 2010, inventory turnover = €/£147,906 ÷ €/£519,271 × 365 = 104 days.

Retailers tend to have a faster inventory turnover than other sectors. In this case, it could be argued that Teckno's inventory turnover in 2011 was rather high at 93 days (although this has 'improved' compared with 2010).

Task 3.2

Part (b)

Report addressed to John Keane

Key Points:

- In 2010 and 2011, Teckno's financial results were mixed.
- The company's return on capital employed fell slightly from 18.6% to 16%. This is due to the fall in operating profit made by the business in 2011. However, a 16% ROCE in 2011 is still a favourable outcome.
- The gross profit margin for Teckno changed only very slightly between the two years. It rose from 44.4% to 45.7%. Although this represents an improvement, it is not significant.
- The net profit margin actually fell over the time period, from 8.6% to 7.7%. Given that gross profit rose very slightly, the net margin suggests that costs have risen a little. Indeed, the statement of comprehensive income indicates that operating expenses rose by nearly €/£20 million.
- Teckno's liquidity seems to have improved considerably. The current ratio rose from 1.15 to 1.44 over the two years. The value in 2011 was nearly in the 1.5 – 2.0 'ideal' range. For a retailer where sales are primarily for cash, a current ratio of 1.44 is very comfortable.
- Teckno has also reduced its gearing from 25.3% to 20.7%. This means that the company has reduced its burden of loans significantly.
- Finally, the company's inventory turnover has improved. In 2010, Teckno sold its inventory every 104 days. In 2011, it was sold every 93 days. This would be a welcome improvement. However, it still seems a little high for a retailer. This might be because Teckno has to hold a great deal of valuable inventory in store.

Task 3.3

There are numerous, often contradictory, ethical issues surrounding the implementation of a policy which utilises lower paid contract staff rather than higher paid salaried employees.

Points might include:
Holinwall's directors have a fiduciary responsibility to act in the best interests of shareholders.

Although, while the directors have to ensure effective operations, they also must consider various ethical obligations or demands (legal and constructive):
- macro level – political, legal, cultural pressures;
- organisational level – corporate social responsibilities of the organisation; and
- individual level.

There are different views on a business's responsibilities. For example:
- separatist view – profit maximisation for the benefit of shareholders; and
- integration view – while a business has to respond to market forces, it also has wider social responsibilities, i.e. to consider the long-term societal implications of its decisions.

Employment practices and the treatment of employees is a major concern for businesses and the public, more so in certain countries and in certain industries.

There is pressure on management to balance the interests of investors, employees, customers and the wider public. While at one level, it can be argued that the company is clearly justified in implementing such a policy, wider considerations, including the 'cost' of negative publicity, may outweigh the more tangible benefits.

Social, environmental and ethical reporting is experiencing an increasing role and prominence. The professional accountancy bodies, including Chartered Accountants Ireland, have issued codes of professional conduct, with the key themes being: integrity; objectivity; professional competence; and confidentiality.

SESSION FOUR

SUGGESTED SOLUTIONS

Task 4.1

Letter addressed to directors of Holinwall.

Key Points:

- In preparing consolidated financial statements, all of the items in the financial statements are added together, as if the parent owned them all, even if the subsidiary is less than 100% owned. For example, the revenue figure in the consolidated statement of comprehensive income is the sum of all the revenues made by group companies, and the inventory figure in the statement of financial position is the sum of all the inventories held by the group members (ignoring the elimination of intercompany sales and inventory profit on unsold inventory).
- When dealing with an associate, only the company's share of profit is taken into account, including its effect on the value of the shareholding: statement of comprehensive income = share of operating profit; statement of financial position = cost of investment + share of post acquisition profits.

Task 4.2

(a)

Holinwall
Consolidated Statement of Comprehensive Income for the Year Ended
31 December 2012

	Holinwall 2012 €/£	Teckno 2012 €/£	ADJUSTMENTS DR €/£	ADJUSTMENTS CR €/£	CONSOL. 2012 €/£
Revenue	26,000,000	950,000	(w3) 100,000		26,850,000
Cost of sales	(12,500,000)	(500,000)		(w3) 90,000	(12,910,000)
Gross profit	13,500,000	450,000			13,940,000
Operating expenses	(8,743,943)	(350,000)	(w1a) 10,000	(w6) 5,000	(9,098,943)
Operating profit	4,756,057	100,000			4,841,057
Finance cost	(82,000)	–	(w1c) 75,100		(157,100)
Profit before tax	4,674,057	100,000			4,683,957
Income tax expense	(850,000)	(40,000)			(890,000)
Profit after tax	3,824,057	60,000			3,793,957
Non-controlling interests	–	–	(w4b) 6,000		(6,000)
	3,824,057	60,000			3,787,957

Holinwall
Consolidated Statement of Financial Position for the Year Ended 31 December 2012

	Holinwall	Teckno	ADJUSTMENTS		CONSOL
	2012	2012	DR	CR	2012
	€/£	€/£	€/£	€/£	€/£
ASSETS					
Non-current Assets					
Land, property, plant, equipment and motor vehicles	7,000,000	180,000	(w1b) 800,000		7,980,000
Goodwill	-	-	(w1b) 311,791	(w1a) 10,000	301,791
Development costs	1,000,000	190,000			1,190,000
	8,000,000	370,000			9,471,791
Current Assets					
Inventory	1,850,000	130,000		(w3) 10,000	1,970,000
Trade receivables	1,300,000	12,000		(w1b) 4,993	1,307,007
Other receivables and prepayments	280,000	-		-	280,000
Current account with Teckno	50,000	-		(w2a) 40,000 (w2b) 10,000	-
Current asset investments	-	240,000			240,000
Bank and cash	200,000	22,003	(w2a) 40,000		262,003
	11,680,000	774,003			13,530,801

Holinwall
Consolidated Statement of Comprehensive Income for the Year Ended
31 December 2010

	Holinwall	Teckno	ADJUSTMENTS		CONSOL
	2012	2012	DR	CR	2012
	€/£	€/£	€/£	€/£	€/£
EQUITY AND LIABILITIES					
Capital and Reserves					
€/£1 ordinary shares			(w1b) 10,709.1		
	600,000	11,899	(w4) 1,189.9	(w1b) 300,000	900,000
Share premium			(w1b) 141,416.1		
	150,000	157,129	(w4) 157,129		439,000
			(w6) 5,000		
Capital redemption reserve	–	706	(w1b) 635.4 (w4) 70.6		–
Retained earnings	7,374,500	243,269	(w5) 279,369		7,338,400
	8,124,500	413,003			8,677,400
Non-controlling interests				(w4a) 120,801	120,801
					8,848,201
Non-current Liabilities					
5% €/£ Cumulative redeemable preference shares	50,000	–			50,000
Bank borrowings	500,000	80,000			580,000
Finance lease	58,250	–			58,250
Other liabilities	–	6,000			6,000
Provisions	200,000	15,000			215,000

Holinwall
Consolidated Statement of Comprehensive Income for the Year Ended
31 December 2010

	Holinwall	Teckno	ADJUSTMENTS		CONSOL.
	2012	2012	DR	CR	2012
	€/£	€/£	€/£	€/£	€/£
Contingent purchase			(w1b) 751,000 (w1c)		
	–	–	75,100		826,100
Current Liabilities					
Bank borrowings	250,000	160,000			410,000
Trade payables	1,300,000	90,000			1,390,000
Other payables and accruals	260,000	–			260,000
Preference dividends	2,000	–			2,000
Taxation	850,000	–			850,000
Finance lease	45,250	–			45,250
Deferred income	40,000	–			40,000
Current account with Holinwall	–	10,000	(w2b) 10,000		–
	11,680,000	774,003			13,530,801

Workings:

1. Purchase of Teckno

Note:
IFRS 3 *Business Combinations* (see Connolly, Chapter 26) was revised in 2008 and the main changes from the 2004 version are:

• Acquisition-related costs

Under IFRS 3 (2004) directly related acquisition costs could be included as part of the cost of acquisition. However, under IFRS 3 (revised 2008) costs incurred in an acquisition are treated as period costs. This means that all acquisition-related costs (e.g. finder's fees; advisory, legal, accounting, valuation, and other professional or consulting fees; and general administrative costs, including the costs of maintaining an internal acquisitions department) should be recognised as period expenses. Costs incurred to issue debt or equity securities should be recognised in accordance with IAS 39 *Financial Instruments: Recognition and Measurement* (see Connolly, Chapter 25).

- Goodwill

Goodwill is the difference between:

- the aggregate of:
  - the acquisition-date fair value of the consideration transferred;
  - the amount of any non-controlling interest in the entity acquired (see below for two measurement options); and
  - in a business combination achieved in stages, the acquisition-date fair value of the acquirer's previously-held equity interest in the entity acquired; and
- the net of the acquisition-date amounts of the identifiable assets acquired and the liabilities assumed, both measured in accordance with IFRS 3 (2008).

If the difference above is positive, the acquirer should recognise the goodwill as an asset. If the difference above is negative, the resulting gain is recognised as a bargain purchase in profit or loss.

- Non-controlling interests (previously referred to as minority interests)

IFRS 3 (2008) has an explicit option, available on a transaction-by-transaction basis, to measure any non-controlling interest in the entity acquired either at fair value (new method) or at the non-controlling interest's proportionate share of the net identifiable assets of the entity acquired (old method). The latter treatment corresponds to the measurement basis in IFRS 3 (2004). For the purpose of measuring non-controlling interest at fair value, it may be possible to determine the acquisition-date fair value on the basis of market prices for the equity shares not held by the acquirer. When a market price for the equity shares is not available because the shares are not publicly-traded, the acquirer must measure the fair value of the non-controlling interest using other valuation techniques.

- Contingent consideration

IFRS 3 requires the consideration for the acquisition to be measured at fair value at the acquisition date. This includes the fair value of any contingent consideration payable. In an exam question, the acquisition date fair value (or how to calculate it) of any contingent consideration would be given. The payment of contingent consideration may be in the form of equity or a liability (issuing a debt instrument or cash) and should be recorded as such under the rules of IAS 32 *Financial Instruments: Presentation*, or other applicable standard. The previous version of IFRS 3 required contingent consideration to be accounted for only if it was probable that it would become payable

Goodwill:	€
Consideration paid by parent	56,000
+ non-controlling interest	12,000
- fair value of the subsidiary's net identifiable assets	(60,000)
Premium on acquisition (positive goodwill)	8,000

(a) Goodwill

		€/£	€/£
Fair value of consideration:	300,000 €/£1 ordinary shares @ €/£1.98		594,000
	Cash payment discounted @ 10%		751,000
			1,345,000
Non-controlling interests	Book value of assets	353,003	
	Revaluation	795,007	
		1,148,010	
	x 10%		114,801
			1,459,801
Fair value of net assets:	Book value	353,003	
	Revaluation (no additional depreciation)	795,007	
			(1,148,010)
Goodwill			311,791
Impairment			(10,000)
			301,791

		DR	CR
		€/£	€/£
DR	Operating expenses – statement of comprehensive income	10,000	
CR	Goodwill – statement of financial position		10,000

(b)   Cost of control

	€/£		€/£
Cost	1,345,000	Share capital (90%)	10,709.10
		Share premium (90%)	141,416.10
		Capital redemption reserve (90%)	635.40
		Retained earnings	164,942.10
		Revaluation (€/£800,000 - €/£4,993) x 90%	715,506.30
	_____	Balance - goodwill	311,791
	1,345,000		1,345,000

DR	Cost of control		€/£1,345,000	
	CR	Share capital		€/£300,000
	CR	Share premium (300,000 x 98c/p)		€/£294,000
	CR	Non-current liabilities - contingent consideration		€/£751,000

DR	Goodwill	€/£311,791	
DR	Share capital	€/£10,709.10	
DR	Share premium	€/£141,416.10	
DR	Capital redemption reserve	€/£635.40	
DR	Retained earnings	€/£164,942.10	
DR	Land	€/£800,000	
	CR	Trade receivables	€/£4,993
	CR	Cost of control	€/£1,345,000
	CR	Non-controlling interests (10% net revaluation)	€/£79,500.70

(c) Deferred consideration

This is a form of debt instrument, and should be shown in the acquiring company's statement of financial position as the investment's cost at the discounted amount. The same amount appears as a non-current liability for deferred consideration. In the statement of comprehensive income, the difference should be treated as a finance cost and charged as an interest expense over the period of the liability so that the annual cost gives a constant rate on the liability carrying amount (10%) (sum of digits may also be used).

Year	Opening balance	Finance cost (10%)	Closing balance
	€/£	€/£	€/£
2012	751,000	75,100	826,100
2013	826,100	82,610	908,710
2014	908,710	90,871	999,581
			(diff. €/£419 rounding)

DR		SCI – Finance cost	€/£75,100	
	CR	Non-current Liabilities		€/£75,100

2. Intercompany accounts

(a) The intercompany accounts differ by €/£40,000, being the cheque in transit from Teckno to Holinwall. Therefore, firstly, reconcile the intercompany accounts:

DR		Cash	€/£40,000	
	CR	Current account with Teckno		€/£40,000

(b) And then cancel intercompany accounts.

3. Intercompany sales and Inventory

Unrealised profit in inventory: 25/125 x €/£100,000 x 50% = €/£10,000

To be eliminated in full against consolidated reserves as Holinwall originally recorded the profit.

DR		Revenue	€/£100,000	
	CR	Cost of sales		€/£90,000
	CR	Inventory		€/£10,000

4. Non-controlling interests

(a) Statement of financial position

	€/£
€/£1 ordinary shares	11,899
Share premium	157,129
Capital redemption reserve	706
Retained earnings	243,269
	413,003
@ 10%	41,300.30
Revaluation (€/£800,000 - €/£4,993) x 10%	79,500.70
	120,801

(b) Statement of comprehensive income
Based on profit after tax of Teckno – €/£60,000 x 10% = €/£6,000

5. Revenue reserves

	€/£
Holinwall	7,374,500
Teckno	243,269
Pre-acquisition reserves (w1b)	(164,942.10)
Goodwill impairment (w1a)	(10,000)
Interest (w1c)	(75,100)
Unrealised profit in inventory (w3)	(10,000)
Non-controlling interests (€/£243,269 x 10%)	(24,326.90)
Share issue expenses (w6)	5,000
	7,338,400

6. Share issue expenses - option to write off against share premium

| DR | | Share premium | €/£5,000 |
| | CR | Operating expenses | €/£5,000 |

(b)

Holinwall
Consolidated Statement of Cash Flows for the Year Ended 31 December 2012

	W	€/£	€/£
Net cash flows from operating activities	1		3,430,278
Cash flows from investing activities			
Purchase of non-current assets	3	(2,980,809)	
Disposal of non-current assets		10,000	
Development costs	8	(103,653)	
Cash taken over with Teckno (incl. current asset investments)		251,736	(2,822,726)
Cash flows from financing activities			
Repayment of borrowings	4	(265,299)	
Capital element of finance leases	5	(15,250)	
Share issue expenses		(5,000)	(285,549)
Increase in cash during the year			322,003
Cash and cash equivalents at start of year			180,000
Cash and cash equivalents at end of year			502,003

Workings:

1. Net cash flows from operating activities		€/£
Operating profit		4,841,057
Goodwill impairment	N1	10,000
Depreciation	N4	410,000
Loss on disposal	N4	120,000
Increase in inventory (€/£1,000,000 – (€/£1,970,000 – €/£128,084))		(841,916)

Increase in receivables (€/£1,460,000 – (€/£1,587,007 – (€/£11,481 – €/£4993))		(120,519)
Increase in payables (€/£1,512,207 – (€/£1,656,000 – €/£108,546))		35,247
Finance costs – borrowings (incl. interest capitalised)	N4 & 5	(75,000)
Finance costs – finance lease	N5	(15,000)
Taxation	W2	(840,000)
Preference dividends paid (prior year) (included in finance costs)		(2,000)
Deferred income	W6	(40,000)
Provisions paid	W7	(51,591)
		3,430,278

2. Taxation	€/£
Opening balance	800,000
Teckno	-
Statement of comprehensive income charge	890,000
Closing balance	(850,000)
Paid	840,000

3. Purchase of land, property, plant, equipment and motor vehicles		€/£
At start of year		4,473,400
Teckno		155,791
Depreciation	N4	(410,000)
Land revaluation	N1	800,000
NBV of disposal	N4	(130,000)
At end of year		(7,980,000)
Increase		(3,090,809)
New finance leases	N4	100,000
Interest capitalised	N4	10,000
		2,980,809

4. Borrowings

	€/£
Opening balance	1,000,000
Closing balance (€/£990,000 – €/£255,299)	(734,701)
	265,299

5. Finance leases

	€/£
Opening balance	18,750
New leases	100,000
Closing balance	(103,500)
Paid	15,250

6. Deferred income

	€/£
Opening balance	80,000
Closing balance	(40,000)
Released to statement of comprehensive income	40,000

7. Provisions

	€/£
Opening balance	250,000
Closing balance (€/£215,000 – €/£16,591)	(198,409)
	51,591

8. Development costs

	€/£
Opening balance	900,000
Closing balance (€/£1,190,000 – €/£186,347)	(1,003,653)
	(103,653)

Task 4.3

Earnings:	€/£
Profit after tax	3,793,957
Non-controlling interests	(6,000)
	3,787,957

Number of Ordinary Shares:
600,000 at start of year   600,000
300,000 issued on 1 January 2012   <u>300,000</u>
                                                          <u>900,000</u>

EPS: <u>3,787,957</u>   = €/£4.21
                                                  900,000